TRAILER BOATS

ALEX ZIDOCK, JR.

Bristol Fashion Publications, Inc.
Rockledge, Florida

Trailer Boats -- *Alex Zidock, Jr.*

Published by Bristol Fashion Publications, Inc.

Copyright © 2000 by Alex Zidock. All rights reserved.

No part of this book may be reproduced or used in any form or by any means-graphic, electronic, mechanical, including photocopying, recording, taping or information storage and retrieval systems-without written permission of the publisher.

BRISTOL FASHION PUBLICATIONS AND THE AUTHOR HAVE MADE EVERY EFFORT TO INSURE THE ACCURACY OF THE INFORMATION PROVIDED IN THIS BOOK BUT ASSUMES NO LIABILITY WHATSOEVER FOR SAID INFORMATION OR THE CONSEQUENCES OF USING THE INFORMATION PROVIDED IN THIS BOOK.

ISBN: 1-892216-32-9
LCCN: 00-131362

Contribution acknowledgments

Cover Design: John P. Kaufman
Cover Photos: Wellcraft, Ranger, Robalo
Information, charts and photos provided by:
The author or the manufacturers as noted and include:
ACDelco, GM Corporation, Grand Blanc, MI
Exide Corporation, Reading, PA
DieHard Batteries, Sears, Roebuck Company
Hoffman Estates, IL
Interstate Batteries, Dallas, TX

DEDICATION

This book is dedicated to my wife JoAnne and daughter Ann, and to my crew who have shared many of my experiences as we knocked around boats and boated together. Friday was crew too.

Trailer Boats -- *Alex Zidock, Jr.*

Trailer Boats -- Alex Zidock, Jr.

TABLE OF CONTENTS

INTRODUCTION   Page 9

CHAPTER ONE   Page 13
    Finding The Right Boat

CHAPTER TWO   Page 25
    Hull Design

CHAPTER THREE   Page 31
    Inflatables

CHAPTER FOUR   Page 35
    Personal Watercraft (PWC)

CHAPTER FIVE   Page 41
    Alternative Boat Ownership

CHAPTER SIX   Page 47
    Boat Trailers

CHAPTER SEVEN   Page 57
    Towing ABC's

CHAPTER EIGHT
Tow Vehicles

Page 65

CHAPTER NINE
Launching & Retrieving

Page 69

CHAPTER TEN
Helmsmanship

Page 77

CHAPTER ELEVEN
All About Gasoline

Page 87

CHAPTER TWELVE
All About Engine Oil

Page 93

CHAPTER THIRTEEN
Batteries

Page 99

CHAPTER FOURTEEN
Propellers

Page 111

CHAPTER FIFTEEN
Bilge Pumps

Page 119

CHAPTER SIXTEEN
Sonar & Fish Finders

Page 127

CHAPTER SEVENTEEN
Fitting Out & Cosmetic Care

Page 133

CHAPTER EIGHTEEN
Pre-season Motor Maintenance

Page 141

CHAPTER NINETEEN   Page 151
Storage - Short & Long Term

CHAPTER TWENTY   Page 157
A To Z Terms and Tips

CHAPTER TWENTY-ONE   Page 179
Tools & Equipment

ABOUT THE AUTHOR   Page 191

Trailer Boats -- Alex Zidock, Jr.

Trailer Boats -- *Alex Zidock, Jr.*

INTRODUCTION

My first boat came as a surprise. Newly married, we thought we would like to have a boat so we could be old salts before the kids came. After all, our neighbors had a boat and they looked forward to the weekends when they could take their boat just north of Philadelphia, Pennsylvania, to the Delaware River for a day on the water. They would water ski, have picnics and seemed to be having more fun on their summer weekends than we were having. Our neighbors invited us boating one weekend, which set the hook even deeper.

"Something small we can easily handle," I relayed to the owner of a boatyard the following weekend as we walked among an array of used boats. This took place in the early 1960s when the majority of used boats on the market were still made of wood and the boatbuilding, fiberglass revolution of 1956 was just taking hold. Some of the boats we looked at were on trailers; others were jacked up, precariously resting on cinder blocks or old railroad ties. The offerings ranged from nearly new (out of our price range) models, to rotting hulks resting on the ground, good only to scavenge for parts.

When we came to a boat near our price range, the sales pitch went something like this: "It just needs a little sanding and varnish, and as you know, you have to do that every year anyway," he said, and I nodded like I knew. But, he assured me, it could look like a real beauty with a little dry-rot patch and some wood screws.

When we left the yard that day, to my surprise, I was towing a 21-foot, teen-aged wooden boat, the best of the bunch in our price range. The boat was strapped to a like-vintage, but miss-matched trailer with a temporary license tag. At the time, I thought the tag was appropriate. The one smart choice was the new 85 h.p. Evinrude outboard motor we added as part of the deal. It was when I finally got the boat in the water that I realized I was not only wet behind the ears, I was also fully immersed in recreational boating. I bolted permanent tags on the trailer. The outboard motor eventually found its way onto another, newer boat.

I've come to believe only the Saint Christopher medal we affixed to a mahogany plank between the cabin doorjamb and the instrument console brought us safely through those early years as the owners of a trailerable boat. Common sense and asking a lot of questions tied for second.

Through the next thirty-five years I've owned everything from an 8-foot aluminum car-topper and a folding Porta-Bote, to aluminum and fiberglass bass and walleye boats and even a 30-foot cabin cruiser we docked at the Atlantic shore. Along the way I've gathered a lot of firsthand experience, learned from other boaters, and I have taken boating courses offered by the U. S. Coast Guard Auxiliary, U. S. Power Squadron and the Pennsylvania Fish and Boat Commission. I've researched and written boating articles since the early 1970s. I've towed boats with a variety of vehicles, and fished from all types of boats in many parts of the country.

Reaching back to when I began my spring boating season scraping, caulking and painting the bottom and teaking the topside, to today's turnkey offerings, I've packed *Trailer Boats* with fact and experience. I have arranged the information so the novice boater can easily follow a course to a safe, pleasurable and satisfying experience on the water. The seasoned boater will find *Trailer Boats* an easy-to-use reference with updated information and technologies. Any old salt will tell you, when it comes to boating, a little knowledge and a lot of common sense go a long way.

Alex Zidock, Jr.

Trailer Boats -- Alex Zidock, Jr.

Trailer Boats -- Alex Zidock, Jr.

CHAPTER ONE
FINDING THE RIGHT BOAT

People usually buy a boat for a specific purpose. A fisherman may be compelled to purchase a boat to fish in a farm pond, inland lake, or a hundred miles out in an ocean. A snow skier may want to extend the sport by buying a boat to water ski. Perhaps a camping family finds taking a boat along would add to their enjoyment by expanding their ability to explore new places. Most times however, the type of boat a family purchases represents a compromise of two or more water related activities. Dad may want a fishing boat, mom may want a cruiser and the kids may be interested in tubing or water skiing. Manufacturers of recreational boats know this, and produce many models of trailerable boats capable of accommodating a variety of boating functions.

When shopping for a new boat, consideration should not only be given to what purpose the boat will be used, but also to *where* the boat will be used. There are a wide variety of larger, yet trailerable, boats that will perform as well in the ocean as in larger bodies of inland waters. These boats may not be suitable for smaller impoundments or shallow rivers. As an example, even if you are sure the boat will be used primarily for fishing, it must be determined whether most of the boat's use will be offshore or on smaller, inland waterways. If the boat is to be used mostly offshore, the tradeoff when used inland will be that the boat may be too large, and it will not ply shallow, inland waters. A boat designed for offshore use may also posses excessive horsepower for inland waters. The bigger boat may be cumbersome to launch and retrieve at smaller launch ramp facilities sometimes associated with inland waters. This could translate into not using the boat as much because of the problems involved in getting it into and out of the water. On the other hand, if the boat is primarily used in smaller inland lakes, it may not be suitable for use offshore, or in large, unprotected bays. The practice of taking a small boat into big water could raise a very serious safety issue.

Larger trailerable boats -- those in the mid and upper twenty-foot range -- are considered to be trailerable in the conventional manner, but are not routinely towed by the average weekend boater. These boats may be taken to an area and docked in one location for an entire boating season. The trailer may be only used for pulling the boat out of the water for repairs and storage.

So, one of the first questions every boater has to ask himself is, "What is "trailerable?" There is no stock answer, because what is trailerable for one person is out of the question for the next. A person who owns a compact car may find the largest boat the vehicle can safely tow is a 14-foot aluminum utility boat with a 10 h.p. outboard engine, a small runabout or an inflatable boat. Another person with a large, mega-powered, 4x4 utility vehicle, might consider towing a fully equipped, 26-foot sport fisherman. The tow vehicle must be one of those variables blended into the decision at boat buying time.

The most widely used boat in America today is about 18 feet long with an outboard engine and is classified as a runabout. They are used for everything from fishing to water skiing and general family cruising. Runabouts come with open bows called bow riders; other runabouts have small, enclosed cabins with canvas camping covers. They are roomy enough for four to six people, have conveniences such as built-in coolers, stereo radios and swim platforms. Runabouts are trailer-friendly and easy to tow, launch and retrieve.

Figure 1
Courtesy of the manufacturer.

Runabout.

Some manufacturers build boats with a very specific function in mind. Certainly everyone is familiar with bass boats, made popular by big-money, bass fishing tournaments operated in recent years by the Bass Anglers Sportsmen's Society (BASS) and other organizations. The bass boat has, aptly, been described, as nothing more than a very sophisticated fishing platform, from which an angler can present a lure to a fish at a variety of water depths and under any circumstance. Bass boats are flat decked with low contoured windshields, and no other obstructions that would snag a fishing line or interfere with casting or catching fish. Bass boats can be made of fiberglass or aluminum. They are equipped with aerated wells to keep fish alive, high casting seats and a host of electronics to find fish. Bass boats have high-powered engines that deliver the fisherman to productive fishing spots in a hurry, so he or she can spend more time fishing than traveling. Speed also allows the tournament fisherman to fish to the last minute and beat the clock back to the dock for weigh-in. However, what one manufacturer might call a "bass boat", could be a design that would also be adequate to tow a water skier.

Boats built specifically for water skiing have hulls designed to produce very little wake, (disturbed water that is produced behind the boat from the combination of the motion of the boats hull and the propeller). On the other hand, some manufacturers have built boats with hulls designed specifically to create certain types of wakes for people who enjoy the fast-growing sport of wakeboarding. Traditional ski boats have inboard motors, but there are models with I/Os. Can you water ski behind a boat with an outboard motor? Yes. In fact, in some manufacturer's lineups, you'll find a "Fish & Ski" model that, again, is a compromise.

Pontoon boats have become very popular among the inland cruising and recreational fishing set. These boats are little more than a fenced-in, flat platform, fastened to two large pontoons, pointed on one end. They are very roomy and stable. Usually the pontoon boat has a roof, but for the most part, it offers no enclosed cabin area. Some pontoon boats are equipped with enough horsepower to pull a water skier or a person on another type of inflatable water toy. Pontoon boats are more suited for flat inland water, where the need is stability, while accommodating larger numbers of passengers. They also make great fishing platforms, but are not designed for speed or maneuverability, as are the bass boats. Some pontoon boats have been referred to as party barges.

Figure 2
Courtesy of the manufacturer.

Pontoon boat.

Figure 3
Courtesy of the manufacturer.

Ski boat.

Rigid hull, inflatable boats (RIBS) are increasing in numbers among first-time boat buyers. These boats evolved from the old-style life rafts, into a highly sophisticated breed of part inflatable and part fiberglass or aluminum constructed boats. Don't discount these boats as being flimsy and easily damaged. Some salvage and marine rescue companies are using RIBS in their everyday work.

Figure 4
Courtesy of the manufacturer.

Ridge bottom inflatable.

Trailer boats also include the futuristic-looking jet boats that followed closely on the wake of the personal watercraft (PWC) craze. Jet boats can best be described as oversized PWC's that are highly maneuverable craft, but ,have the capacity to hold more people.

In the early days of recreational boating, until about 1956, most boats were made of wood. Fiberglass and aluminum are the popular choices today. Both of these construction materials are much lighter than wood and allow larger boats to be carried on trailers. Today's modern hull constructions are also stronger than wood and are more easily maintained. However, if a boater has a flare for the unusual, antique wooden boats are still available, and refurbished models appear at classic boat shows, or are available through antique boats clubs. A fine example of classic wooden boats is the display at the

Trailer Boats -- *Alex Zidock, Jr.*

Antique Boat Museum in Clayton, New York, located in the Thousand Islands Region of the Empire state. Because it has become the center for antique boats, it is a good place to begin a search for an old wooden boat. If you like the style of old boats and the look of wood, but want the easy maintenance of fiberglass, there are companies that make fiberglass boats that replicate the texture and appearance of wood. But as any old salt will tell you, while today's plastic boatbuilding materials have certain advantages, nothing rides like a wooden boat.

Boats, no matter what the construction, come in all types of configurations. In the search for a trailerable boat the buyer must determine if an open boat, or one with an enclosed cabin better suits the need. Many times a manufacturer will make several, trailerable model variations on one hull design. They will range from a basic bare-bones fishing boat with a center console, to a cabin cruiser with a plush interior, built-in head, galley and even sleeping berths.

Depending on how and where you intend to use your boat, will have an effect on the type of power you choose to propel your boat. Outboard motors are the most popular. An outboard motor hangs on the outside of the boat from the transom, and takes up no space in the boat, except for the fuel tanks. However, some smaller engines, usually up to 5 h.p., even have self-contained fuel tanks. Some engines can be lifted on and off the transom by one person for service and indoor storage, when the boat is not in use. Others are so large, a special hoist must be used to remove the motor from the boat. Usually motors of this size remain on the boat during repairs and storage. Outboard motors are also available with the standard propeller, or with a jet-drive. Jet drives suck water into the lower unit of the motor and expel it with great force. There is usually little difference in the actual engine, between propeller driven or jet drive motor boats. Boats equipped with jet-drives are ideal for shallow water operation but are not as efficient as propeller driven boats. Also, they are not as maneuverable at slower speeds as a boat with a propeller engine.

Hi-bred boats built for the serious water skier, usually have inboard engines where the propeller is connected to the motor with a straight, rigid shaft which protrudes from the bottom of the boat. The boat is steered by means of a rudder as opposed to moving the propeller from side to side, as happens with the outboard or inboard/outboard (I/O) units.

The I/O is a combination of an inboard motor with an outdrive gear case that protrudes from the bottom of the transom. The lower unit of this type of motor is very similar to the lower unit on an outboard motor.

Power selection in outboard engines is available in newer-version, two-stroke technology, offering fuel injection and other environmentally friendly options. However, there has been much progress made in outboard engines in, the more environmentally compatible, four-stroke technologies. Two-stroke engines require oil be mixed with the gasoline before ignition. In the older technology, the oil was mixed directly with the gasoline in the same tank. Oil injection models now allow oil to be held in a separate reservoir, then injected, in precise amounts, into the cylinders at the exact time of ignition. This lubricates the piston rings and other internal engine parts. For the most part, the combustion in the cylinder is hot enough to burn the fuel and most of the oil.

Four stroke engines are based on the same principals as automobile engines. The oil is never mixed burnt with the gasoline in the combustion chamber, so there is less pollution in the exhaust. The piston rings keep the oil on one side of the cylinder and the gasoline on the other. The oil lubricates the piston rings, which in turn, forms a seal to maintain compression in the cylinders and also prevents the gasoline from mixing with the oil. Four-stoke engines are cleaner burning since the exhaust only contains the emissions from the burned gasoline. The tradeoff here is that the four-stroke engines are generally heavier, pound to horsepower, than their two-stroke cousins.

If you have access to the Internet, you can begin your search for a boat right at home. Almost all boat manufacturers have web sites with their models and accessories listed. But, once you've narrowed your choices, you need to get out and see the boats first hand. Boat shows are a great place to see many types of boats in one place, and many dealers offer test rides at boat shows. Attend more than one boat show, since some dealers may exhibit at one show but not the other. Find more than one boat dealer in your area where you can sit down and discuss the items on your boat wish list. Many dealers have Demo Days, where they invite the general public to a picnic-type event. They provide food, refreshment and a wide selection of boats to test-drive. Take advantage of all opportunities to see boats on land and in the water. Don't be afraid to talk to friends who own boats, and get their advice. If you shop carefully, you will purchase the boat suited to fit your needs, and provide countless hours of satisfaction and pleasure.

Don't overlook the used boat market. It is a fact, that most boats sold in the United States are driveway deals. New or used you should approach the initial boat buying process the same way. Make a list of what you want in a boat, and then search the newspaper and the Internet for something that comes close. However, there are as many things to be concerned with when you buy a used boat, as when you buy a used automobile or truck. As an example, there is a glut of personal watercraft

Trailer Boats -- Alex Zidock, Jr.

(PWC) in the used boat marketplace right now for several reasons. First of all, peak sales of PWC took place in the mid-1990s when, in most states, there were no specific laws concerning age or education requirements for the operators. Since then, some states have passed laws restricting operators who were below a certain age, or who have not passed a safe boating course. Rather than comply, some owners are just selling their PWC. Secondly, during the heyday of PWCs several traditional boat manufacturers and manufacturers of snowmobiles and all terrain vehicles began producing their own brand of PWC. As the sales of PWCs dropped in the late 1990's, several manufacturers stopped producing the craft. Owners of those, no-longer-in-production models want to sell them before they become totally, obsolete and parts become scarce. No matter what type used boat you may look at, do your homework before you buy. Follow the axiom, 'buyer beware.'

For the most part, purchasing a boat is an easy process that should begin with a notebook and a pen. Start with a budget, taking into consideration, the type and amount of financing you can afford. You need to be concerned, not only with the base price of a boat, but with the cost of the accessories you will want to add, or the repairs you may have to put into a used boat. Then make a list of all of the reasons why you want to buy a boat, and the activities you, your family, friends, and your new boat will do together. Consider the size and weight your tow vehicle will handle. Make a list of places and types of water on which you will use the boat, and then make a list of all of the other concerns you have about boat ownership. Take your notebook with you every time you look for a boat. Make a lot of notes you can compare later when you get home.

Buying the right boat the first time takes a lot less effort than buying the wrong boat and then trying to sell or trade it later because it doesn't fit your needs. There is one basic rule that will keep you out of trouble on land or on the water. It is applicable from when you first get the idea you want to buy a boat, until you sell your boat. If you follow the rule faithfully it will serve you faithfully all through your boating life. BE PREPARED!

Trailer Boats -- *Alex Zidock, Jr.*

CHAPTER TWO
HULL DESIGN

Early in our nautical history, boats were powered by wind or oars. It didn't take long for boat builders to find boats went faster, and were easier to maneuver, if the bow was pointed. They soon discovered that by lowering the center of gravity, ships with high sail masts had better balance, and the low center of gravity helped keep the boat upright, even in foul weather. Many times, neatly squared rocks were piled in the center of the large sailing ships to hold the ship lower in the water for more stability. In fact, many of the square rocks once used for ballast can still be seen in some of our early seaport cities, like Philadelphia where the rocks were used to build city streets. These early boats were constructed with displacement hulls. This means the hull would push through the water, and displace the same amount of water as the weight of the hull and its cargo. Just sitting in the water, or underway, the displacement hull's relationship to the amount of water displaced, remains the same.

Generally, the displacement hull was the most popular design with early boats, and in full, or in part, is still used in some designs of recreational boats today. Boats with complete displacement hulls are characterized as heavier and slower than boats with partial or complete planing hulls. The proper propeller for a displacement hull is one with a lower than normal pitch.

With the advent of mechanical power and the

ability to push boats faster, came boats with "planing" hulls. The hull is constructed so the boat is partially lifted out of the water and skims on the surface. However, when a planing hull is not underway, it reverts to the characteristics of a displacement hull. It's sometimes difficult to tell the difference between the two, but there are slight differences. Most boats are designed with properties of each type of hull. However, even with the slightest movement, the planing hull, reacting to the water, will immediately change its action from displacement characteristic at rest, to planing ability. Propellers on boats with planing hulls sometimes are not fully submerged, and thus need to provide holding ability, as well as have a higher pitch and rake because of higher top-end speeds the propeller achieves. The propeller needs to be able to 'bite' into the water, restraining the engine from going over the manufacturer's recommended RPM.

Hull design has a lot to do with the ability of any boat to perform the task for which it was built. Throughout our various chapters in this book, we talk about compromise. The same is true when it comes to hulls and hull design, and the boat manufacturer's ability to satisfy as many people as possible with one design. A cruiser may be built with a deep vee forward to allow the boat to achieve higher speeds by slicing through the waves and water. It may have a flat bottom near the transom to add stability at rest and planing when in motion.

One thing you can say about completely flat bottom boats is, that with their large bottom area, the boat is very stable in nice weather and calm, flat water. Flat bottom boats can have a sharply pointed bow, but many newer ones are of the Jon boat design, with a flat, broad bow area. The later design is very stable in shallow water and is a great boat where weeds are encountered and the boat can plow right over top. With their planing hull, aluminum Jon boats can get up on plane very quickly, offering a smooth ride with a low horsepower motor. In bad weather, the Jon boat is sometimes tough to handle. In rough water the hull has a tendency to 'slap' the water with each rise and fall of the bow. Most flat bottom boats with displacement hulls are limited to low horsepower motors.

The round-bottom boat has a displacement hull and is generally used for dinghies, tenders and sometimes car-top boats. This style boat is easier to maneuver at slow speeds than the flat-bottom boat.

The V-bottom boat is the most common hull design. Most manufacturers of boats being built today use modifications of this design. This design offers a good ride in rough water, as the pointed bow slices forward through the water, and the V shaped bottom softens the up and down movement of the boat. The degree of the angle of the V is called deadrise. As the V shape extends to the back of the boat it usually flattens out until it all but disappears at the transom. Some V bottom boats have a flat surface at the very bottom called a pad. This pad allows a little more planing surface at the sacrifice of a little softness in the ride. But this addition of the 'pad' on the keel increases top speed.

Boats that are a distinct modification of the 'V' bottom are called tri-hulls and cathedral hulls. The cathedral hull boat is the traditional V hull with additional outside hulls. Turn it upside down and it looks like a cathedral with one main spire and two side spires. This design is more stable than the 'V' bottom at rest, but it gives a rougher ride in choppy water due to the increased surface area at the bow of the boat.

Tunnel boats have been designed to trap a cushion of air beneath the hull to reduce drag on the outside hulls. This design is different than a catamaran bottom, because the inner edges of the outside hulls have sharp corners to improve the handling of these boats at very high speeds. Many race boats are constructed with tunnel hulls, which are sometimes called hydroplanes.

Very popular, in some portions of the country, are pontoon boats. And just as the name implies, the pontoon boat is a flat, raised deck, supported with two outer hulls (pontoons), usually constructed of aluminum. These boats combine a lot of features of other boats. They ride very dry since the deck is raised above the floats. They are stable, and with the transom mounted aft of the deck, they are easy to maneuver with an outboard motor.

The boater looking for all-around use, can make almost any hull design work for many water conditions. But, in the broadest markets, hull design is a continual research and development project. In specific niche markets, like water skiing, and now in the fastest growing of the water sports markets, wake boarding, the competition for better hulls makes choosing one over the other a tough job.

To show how complicated and intricate the designs of boat hulls can be, Correct Craft's TWC (Total Wake Control) hull features a mix of hull design technology. The description of this new hull design says, the bottom is made up of longitudinal strakes, anti sway roll, spray rails, ramping vents, air side cutouts and bow lifting strakes, all of which work harmoniously to create a spectacular wake shape, ramp angle, lip and curl for an incredible ride.

Figure 5
Courtesy of the manufacturer.

The power catamaran has become a popular design.

Trailer Boats -- Alex Zidock, Jr.

CHAPTER THREE
INFLATABLES

If inflatable boats were available when Captain Ahab chased Moby Dick, perhaps that whale of a tale would have taken a different twist. Jacques-Yves Cousteau brought air-filled boats into our living rooms, with television scenes of Zodiacs nestled alongside the *Calypso* in all types of foreign environments. The U.S. Navy Seals and the U.S. Coast Guard use them, transoceanic survivors proved them, commercial salvage companies can't destroy them, and yet, until recently the general U.S. boater ignored them as serious boats. But now a new tide of development has fathered the idea that maybe inflatable boats are more than tenders to the yachting world. Inflatable boats have become trendy; they're even being considered as the family primary boat.

Inflatable boats now offer another option to traditional fiberglass and aluminum boats to buyers shopping for primary boats. The evolution of the Rigid-Hull Inflatable Boat (RIB) and the air-floor or air-deck, has opened a whole new market to the manufacturers of inflatable boats. These products were recognized as dinghies and tenders for larger craft.

Inflatable boats are produced in two categories. There is the traditional inflatable that may have a soft floor, wood or fiberglass roll-up or interlocking flooring system, or the newest advancement, the hard inflatable floor. Most boats in this group are frequently deflated, and fold up into a small package for storage, transportation in small compartments on larger boats, automobile trunks or small trailers.

RIBs make up the second category. As the name implies, the hull is usually made of one-piece formed fiberglass, or aluminum, and is usually moved about on land with a trailer. The deck and passenger accommodations are designed as one integral piece, particularly when fiberglass is used. The tubes are not deflated, except possibly, for shipping from the factory, and for long-term storage. In larger boats, the tubes are 'welded' or fastened to the hull, and in most cases, are inseparable from the hull.

To keep the inflatable boats affordable, convenient to use and tough, manufacturers sometimes use polyethylene instead of fiberglass for the hull. Systems were developed in smaller RIBS so the tubes can be easily detachable from the deep 'V' hull for storage or repairs. The tube part of an inflatable boat is made of tough tear-resistant fabric.

The inflatable boat has always been ideal as a tender to a larger boat because of its flexible sides, which has advantages, even in today's niche markets. The routine procedure of getting the rubber boat on and off the mother ship or coming along side to pick up and discharge passengers, prevented damage caused by a conventional, fiberglass or aluminum hull.

Inflatable boats are more comfortable on the water because the tubes form to the water surface. They are much lighter than fiberglass sport boats or runabouts making them easier to move short distances over land or obstacles. In the water think of the tubes as a shock absorber. On a rough sea the RIBs are more comfortable than conventional boats because the hull and the tubes take the shape of the waves. The V hull cuts the water pushing the spray under the large tubes and sending it out in a more horizontal line, which helps keep the passengers dry.

There are many advantages to owning an inflatable boat. Because the buoyancy is due to air and not material, the inflatable boat can carry a heavier payload than a fiberglass boat of comparative size. And because the boat is lighter, it needs less horsepower. Less horsepower means a smaller engine and less fuel cost, while maintaining overall boat performance.

An 8-foot inflatable boat will accept a 5 h.p. outboard, and can provide great performance in a small body of water. A larger, 23-foot RIB fitted with a 66 gallon fuel tank and a 17-gallon fresh water tank, would perform well as a sport boat, ski boat or fishing boat in a much larger body of water. It would operate very well with twin, 75 h.p. outboards. A single, 200 h.p. outboard engine on the same boat will produce 57 mph.

RIBs are becoming more customer friendly. With the addition of soft seats, radios, navigation lights and all the accessories of traditional boats, they maintain a high degree of safety and stability. Inflatable boats are made from about eight feet to over 35 feet in length. They can be powered with most conventional power plants, including diesel and jet drive engines.

Trailer Boats -- Alex Zidock, Jr.

Figure 6
Courtesy of the manufacturer.

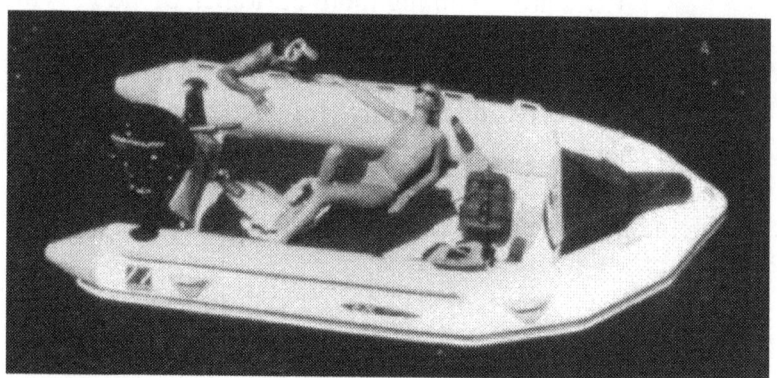

Figure 7
Courtesy of the manufacturer.

Two views of ridge bottom inflatables.

Trailer Boats -- Alex Zidock, Jr.

CHAPTER FOUR
PERSONAL WATERCRAFT (PWC)

According to the United States Coast Guard's description and regulations, Personal Watercraft (PWC) are indeed classified as boats. In their eyes they are treated as boats where boating laws and construction are concerned. For the last several years PWC's were among the fastest growing segment of the boating industry, reaching peak sales in the mid-1990's. When sales were on the upswing, several traditional boat manufacturers took advantage of the PWC's popularity and began producing their own line of boats. In recent years, and as their popularity dropped, some of those same manufacturers have discontinued producing their models. Other manufacturers continue to put money into research and development, refining PWC's to challenge the next generation of owners.

PWC's are attractions of a niche group of people who seek personal freedom and/or the excitement of speed on the water. PWC's have found a permanent place among water-based police and rescue teams. The PWC's attraction to the general boating public seems no different than that of land-bound motorcycles, snowmobiles or all-terrain vehicles (ATV's).

Unfortunately, with the speed and excitement of the PWC, comes a danger to both the rider, and others who may be using the same waterway. While PWC's still make up only a small percentage of the boats registered nationally, PWC's are involved in more accidents than all other types of boats.

It's not that these small boats are particularly dangerous themselves. The danger arises from irresponsible operation. The proportionally high rate of accidents, injuries and deaths that have occurred across the country are due mostly, to inexperienced operators. A study of PWC owners released by the Personal Watercraft Industry Association (PWIA) states that, "On a typical riding day, an average of six or seven different people operated the watercraft." In most cases, drivers have little or no training in navigation, or the rules-of-the-road, observed by more experienced boaters. The same things that make the PWC exciting and fun to ride; speed, maneuverability and the disregard of rules, also make it a dangerous activity.

Figure 8
Courtesy of the manufacturer.

Students are learning PWC safety.

Trailer Boats -- Alex Zidock, Jr.

Boating safety courses may not be the complete answer to safer operation of PWC's, but will help. In states with mandatory education, the operators of PWC's dropped dramatically, from the average of 6 or 7 operators per day, to just 3. In those states, operators are usually owners and immediate members of their family, who have all taken a safe boating course. Operators are usually more careful if they own the machine. While parents can reprimand their children for misuse, adults may feel uncomfortable reprimanding a visiting friend operating their PWC in an unsafe manor. People who only, occasionally, have the opportunity to operate a PWC may not take the time to attend a boating safety course. Mandatory education lowers the number of inexperienced operators, which reduces problems and complaints handled, by marine police officers.

While there is a trend among states to promote safer operation through rule making, other national and state laws are aimed at manufacturers to produce quieter and less polluting machines.

Sound is more of an annoying factor than a safety factor. Conventional, two-stroke, outboard boat motors push exhausts out through the propeller, which is underwater and muffles the sound. On the other hand, PWC's scream when the boat jumps a wake and the exhaust and jet pump are both out of the water. The high pitch sound that annoys everyone, occurs when the throttled-up, two-stroke engine momentarily races the jet pump, which dramatically increases the noise.

The Environmental Protection Agency (EPA) has directed all marine, motor manufacturers to cut hydrocarbon emission in new motors up to 80 percent by the year 2006. Direct fuel injection and other improvements have lead to cleaner burning, two-stroke, marine engines. These new engines will not only cut pollution, but address the sound problems as well. Many

Trailer Boats -- *Alex Zidock, Jr.*

marine, motor manufacturers have introduced four-stroke technology into their outboard motor lineup in recent years. Four-stroke engines which burn straight gasoline, weigh more than their equivalent, two-stroke cousins. Because of present design, four-stroke engines cannot be turned up-side-down and still continue to operate. But that's just the present and there is no doubt future technology will overcome that characteristic. It's a fun machine, and for the more spirited, PWC's are designed to be ridden hard, dumped over and even drenched occasionally. After all, isn't that the attraction?

For the most part, PWC operation is regulated nationally by the same laws that govern other small boats. Some regional and state laws may vary, but, according to the U.S. Coast Guard, PWC's fall into the category of boats under 16 feet. As such, they must follow the same rules of the road assigned to traditional boats. However, the Coast Guard has relaxed certain regulations as they apply to technical construction standards, including fuel tanks, flotation and ventilation designs of PWC's.

Where accident reporting is concerned, the U.S. Coast Guard still lumps PWC figures with all traditionally designed boats. Boat manufacturers claim this has caused an unrealistic picture as to safety of traditional boating. They say these skewed reports frighten potential buyers of family pleasure boats, and small fishing boats.

The Personal Watercraft Industry Association (PWIA) has produced safety videos and safety materials that have been adopted by the Coast Guard Auxiliary and the Power Squadrons. They are now used in many states as part of boating safety education courses. In a growing number of states, a certificate showing the operator has successfully completed a safe boating course is mandatory for legal operation of a PWC.

Trailer Boats -- *Alex Zidock, Jr.*

According to a study by the PWIA, the average age of a PWC owner is 41, and two-thirds are 35 years and older. The average household income of owners is about $96,000, 71 percent of owners are married, and 77 percent have white-collar jobs. The study also found the average PWC owner has experience riding their craft for more than four years. More than two-thirds of the owners indicate they have owned a powerboat of some type prior to buying their first PWC. With the advent of two and three seater PWC models, families use the boats for family outings. While the craft may not be suitable to use as a fishing platform, many anglers are finding that the shallow-running PWC can get them to an unreachable shoreline for bank fishing or wading. It has brought many nature-lovers closer to nature and wildlife when used to tour out-of-the-way places and secluded coves.

Personal Watercraft are here to stay. The root of this love/hate relationship will always depend on where you sit. Before you make a decision on whether you want to own a PWC, plant your bottom on the seat of a PWC and clamp down on the throttle. If you have a low mentality, very soon you too could be on the receiving end of a shaking fist. But, once you understand the high-performance PWC is still a boat, and all rules of boating apply, you'll do all right. If you respect the rights of others, you will join the large number of people who have found a PWC not only to be exhilarating, but also a new way to access and enjoy the many lakes and rivers our nation has to offer.

Trailer Boats -- Alex Zidock, Jr.

CHAPTER FIVE
ALTERNATIVE BOAT OWNERSHIP

When someone considers getting into boating, the first natural thought that comes to mind is buying a boat outright. There are alternative methods without all the hassle of self-ownership.

There are many cases where partnerships are created for the specific purpose of buying a boat. An agreement is drawn up and signed by each party, outlining all the aspects of the partnership. Even though you begin the partnership with two, three, four or more 'owners' it's best to put everything in writing and have the final document notarized. Each party should receive a copy of the signed document.

A few of the details that must be worked out are how and when each will pay his share of the costs for the initial purchase and for upkeep. When each party will have the opportunity to use the boat is another big factor that has to be worked out. While a multi-owner partnership won't work for most, it has worked well under certain circumstances.

I have a friend who moved to Key West several years ago. One of the first things he did was purchase a new boat. After a few years he realized, because of other activities, he was using the boat less and less. He found there were other guys in the community experiencing the same situation. They all wanted a boat at their disposal but considering the number of days they used their boats each year, the cost of upkeep and storage, was a considerable sum of money. While each could afford to own their own boat, they were all retired businessmen who knew there had to be a better way. One day they got together and worked out an 'arrangement.' Each sold his own boat and together they went boat shopping. It wasn't long before all five 'buddies' were fishing together and having more fun than when they each owned their own boat. Their arrangement consisted of a five-way partnership. They each put up one-fifth of the original price to buy and outfit the boat with electronics and all the other things they agreed the boat needed. Each month they pay a nominal amount for upkeep, slip rent insurance and storage. One guy handles all of the paperwork involved in the partnership. They put a little of that monthly payment into a holding account for future or emergency use. They all don't fish on the boat at one time, so the days someone is going out, anyone who joins him for the day chips in for gas and bait. According to my friend, the arrangement has been working well for four or five years. In fact, they're considering trading in the old boat for a newer one.

  Then there are some companies offering a more formal program. The program offers a 'share' in a certain style and size boat. The customer has use of the boat for a certain amount of days a year depending on the boat and share size. The customer can keep that share and enjoy all the benefits of boat ownership as long as they want, or sell the share back to the company, or to anyone else for any price at any time. This situation is much like time-share condominiums.

  Another company has a modified, fractional boat ownership program where customers purchase a share in a boat, pay a monthly service fee and a per hour operating fee, and the company provides everything else including the fuel. The customer does not have an equity interest in the boat, but this kind of program offers yet another type of 'ownership.' The company handles all the scheduling and paperwork as part of the monthly service fee. The company has a fleet of boats that are all the same. Same model, same size and same accomodations. Only the color may be different. The customer gets whatever boat is available at the time.

Following the lead of the automotive and aircraft industries, other boat manufacturers have announced leasing programs through their individual dealerships. This has grown out of the research that to sell boats, boat builders have to give boating to the people the way the people want to have it. Some of the advantages of leasing are that you can lease a boat for a year or even a couple of years and turn it in for a new model. Very similar to what some car owners are doing.

Most leasing programs follow simple automobile leasing principles. If a customer would rather lease a boat, he or she selects the boat and options and agrees to the final price. The dealer sells the boat to the leasing company, and the leasing company leases the boat to the customer. The dealer gets a check from the leasing company, which includes the sales person's commission, just as would happen with conventional automobile financing. The customer's monthly payments are determined on the total price of the boat, less the cost of the initial down payment.

A very creditworthy individual may not be required to put any money down, while others may reduce their monthly payment with an initial down payment. The customer may lease for one, two or three years. Depending on the lease and the leasing company, at the end of the period the customer has four choices; trade it, buy it, sell it or upgrade it. With some companies the customer may even choose to lease the same boat.

Or, if the customer determines boating does not fit the lifestyle, at the end of the lease the customer may just walk away. By the same token the dealer who leased the boat has choices. He may take the boat back and put it in his used boat lot where he can release the boat to a new customer, or the dealer can sell the boat outright. If the boat is too beat up, he can ship the boat back to the manufacturer and leave it up to the manufacturer to dispose of it.

There is a financing difference in leasing a boat than a car. Automobile companies are huge and have unlimited money to spend to help people get into one of their cars. So automobile companies use their own leasing company to lease cars. Most boat manufacturers, on the other hand, must look to outside leasing companies for money, so you can usually expect to pay higher interest rates.

While about 40 percent of all automobiles on the road today are leased, don't look to every boat dealer to have a leasing program.

Fractional ownership, as another company calls their multiple-owner program, is an advanced concept, heretofore used primarily in the aviation industry, where it has been highly successful. The concept sells an equity share, which means the people buying a share in one of the companies boats actually own the boat, they can enjoy the tax benefits allowed under the law, and can realize the proceeds of the sale of that share. The share can be as small as one-eighth, or even one-sixteenth of the ownership of a boat.

While there are opportunities to buy into a program that offers low-cost, limited use of a boat throughout the country, most untraditional types of ownership are offered only in pockets of high boat use and ownership. Most companies setting up this kind of program benefit from being in the south, where boat usage is a year-round opportunity.

On the other hand, there are some builders who offer leasing programs anywhere in the country. As long as theirs is the type of boat you want, then maybe it's a good deal for you.

Like my friend in Key West, you can set up your own program, as long as you know beforehand, that type of ownership is just an alternative to being the captain of your own destiny.

Trailer Boats -- Alex Zidock, Jr.

CHAPTER SIX
BOAT TRAILERS

The least expensive component of the trailer boating triangle could make the difference between a successful boat outing, and the failure to even get near the water. The boat trailer has a big job, and with little care and maintenance it will last as long as the boat. We buy boats because we *want* them, but we buy boat trailers because we *need* them. Yet, there is far less concern about the quality of the trailer we purchase to haul our very expensive boats safely and securely over thousands of miles. We get in our costly tow vehicles equipped with special towing packages, upgraded suspension, transmission coolers and special load-supporting hitches and take off. We pull our trailers over super-fast expressways, then down some of the worst back-road terrain to get to some off-the-beaten-track fishing hole. At road's end we soak the trailer at a muddy launch ramp or in salt water, and wonder why the trailer breaks down. I guess it's just our nature to assume the trailer was built to take that kind of punishment.

Today, many manufacturers sell their boats as packages. That's good for the novice boater who does not have the experience to choose the best engine or the best trailer for that pretty, new boat he or she sees on the showroom floor. For many the decision may not have to be made of which trailer is best for the boat. Even at that, once the package gets home and the neighbors come over to inspect the new toy, it's the sleek lines of the boat and husky horsepower that gets all of the ooohs and aaahs. As years go by, it seems the attention never shifts, and while the boat and motor get all the attention the trailer just does its job until it breaks down.

Before we get into trailer maintenance lets explore the different types of trailers available. After all, you may decide to purchase a new boat that does not come with a trailer as a package or you may opt for a used boat that may not have a trailer.

Modern trailers are made of steel, aluminum or a combination of both. The pieces are welded and bolted together. Trailers come in a variety of sizes and configurations to handle the many types of boats available across the country. Some trailers have rollers strategically placed to support the boat at its heavy load points. Usually, these rollers are adjustable and can be tilted from side to side or raised and lowered. Other trailers have 2x4-inch or 2x6-inch pieces of wood laid on their side and covered with indoor/outdoor carpeting. These are called bunks. With some hull configurations, the bunk trailers distribute the weight of the boat over a wider area, but boats on bunk trailers must be floated on and off the trailer. Boats on trailers with rollers can be rolled off and on the trailer and are easier to use in shallow water. Either type of trailer support system works well. If a trailer is being purchased separately from the boat, the boat manufacturer's recommendation should be taken into consideration before the trailer is purchased. The worst mistake a boater can make is to purchase a used trailer because the 'price is right', not because it fits the load-need of the boat it will support.

Depending on the load it will carry, boat trailers come with one, two or even three axles. Some have their own braking system. Depending on the size of the load and the design of the trailer some trailers have larger hitch couplers than others. This is crucial, but easy to correct by exchanging the hitch ball on the tow vehicle to match the socket size of the trailer coupler. Each coupler and each hitch is marked. As an example you do not want to use a coupler marked '2-inches' on a hitch ball that is marked '1-5/8-inches.'

Most new boat trailers are manufactured with the correct lighting configuration to pass all state requirements. Trailers manufactured in America follow the American lighting system. That means that there is only one wire that connects the turn signals and stoplights to the tow vehicle. Tow vehicles manufactured in foreign countries use separate wires for the turn signals (yellow or amber lenses) and stop lights (red lenses). If the tow vehicle is one of foreign manufacture a converter may be needed to make the running lights, brake lights and turn signals work correctly. Any good marine dealer can provide the converter and connection information.

Load weight and proper load distribution are important for safe and efficient hauling. Every trailer should have a plate on the tongue listing the Gross Vehicle Weight Rating (GVWR) which tells the operator how much weight the trailer is designed to handle safely. The total weight of the boat, with a full tank of gas, all accessories and anything else 'stowed' in the boat while the boat is being towed, should not exceed the GVWR listed on the trailer plate.

Boat trailers are made so a boat may be moved forward or back on the trailer for better weight distribution. For best handling, the tongue of the trailer should transfer some of the total weight to the tow vehicle at the hitch. Since the design of the trailer has much to do with weight distribution, it is nearly impossible to determine the proper tongue weight in every instance. As a general rule, boat trailers may have only 5% to 10% of the total weight of the boat supported at the tongue. If the weight of the boat exceeds the recommended hitch weight, a weight-distributing hitch may be a necessity for safe towing. The easy way to measure tongue weight is to place a bathroom scale under the coupler or the trailer jack, at its normal towing height.

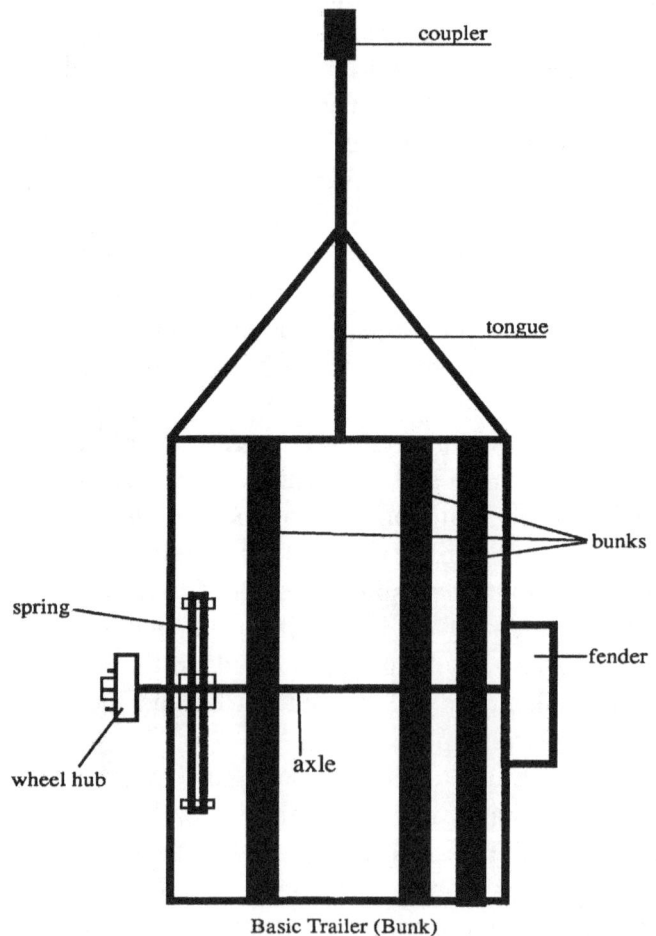

Basic Trailer (Bunk)

Figure 9
Bunk trailer.

Trailer Boats -- Alex Zidock, Jr.

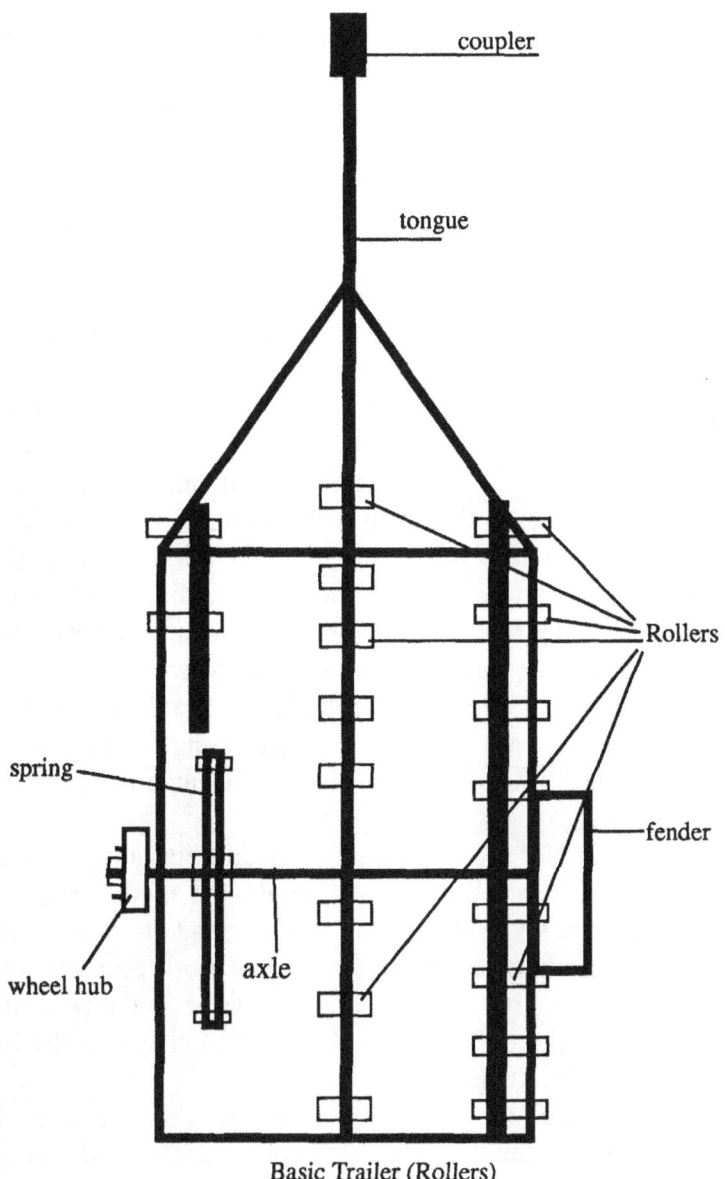

Figure 10
Roller trailer.

Trailer Boats -- *Alex Zidock, Jr.*

If the dealer has not already set up your boat/trailer package, you can do it yourself. To determine the best position for your boat on the trailer, attach the trailer with boat to the tow vehicle. Drive it a short distance, increasing to legal driving speeds. Continue on roads with higher speed limits as long as you don't get any trailer sway, or experience any other unsafe driving conditions. If the trailer sways it means there is too little or too much weight on the tongue. (The boat is too far back or too far forward on the trailer). If the tow vehicle feels as though it is being pushed around at the back end it means there is too much weight on the tongue. A visual inspection may show the back end of the tow vehicle is pushed down. This is certainly an indication there is too much weight on the tongue. Conversely, if the back of the tow vehicle is being held up in the air, it's easy to see the boat is too far back on the trailer. Adjust the boat on the trailer by moving the bow stop forward or backward until the sway stops. This is a trial and error process, but once you get it right, the trailer will follow the tow vehicle with ease and make driving the rig effortless. The experience of a good marine mechanic can go a long way to help.

Trailer maintenance is constant but not as bad as it seems. The trailer boater should get in the habit of completing a visual inspection before and after each trip. Glance at the tires, make sure lights work properly and the lenses are not cracked or full of water. Is the boat still nestled to the trailer as it's supposed to be? Does the rig generally look right?

Once in a while, when the boat has been unloaded, check the rollers or bunks. Take a good look at the weld joints to make sure the weld has not cracked. Follow the wires from the hitch connection to all of the lights looking for indications of rubbing or wear.

A good time to inspect the hitch is when the boat

and tow vehicle are not connected. Every time, before you lower the coupler onto the ball, check the nut holding the ball to the hitch. Vibration may cause the large nut on the ball to loosen. There should be lock washer on the threaded shaft, and Lock-Tite liquid before the nut is installed. It's a great idea to carry a wrench to fit this nut in a convenient place. If you are traveling long distance, every time you stop for gas, at a rest stop or for the night, the coupler-hitch should be checked. Remember that this little point of connection is where the action is. If the hitch comes loose you're asking for heaps of trouble that could cause disaster and a crash.

There are several manufacturers of hitch balls, but the solid, one-piece forged designs are the best. At least once a year, perhaps at the beginning of your boating season, the ball should be removed and the ball hole in the hitch should be inspected. If the hole begins to elongate, drill a larger hole to accommodate a ball with a larger threaded shaft, or replace the hitch.

Safety chains are required in most states. USE THEM! Chains should be attached to the trailer tongue and to the frame of the tow vehicle. It's best not to weld the chains to either side, instead just loop the chains over the frame and put a bolt through the links. Make sure the chains are long enough so they don't bind when you make a sharp turn. Make sure the chains are short enough so they don't drag on the ground. The main thing is to fasten the chains in a way so if the hitch and coupler come undone, the chains will prevent you from loosing the trailer altogether.

Wheels and tires are also very important. Always carry a spare tire and check it regularly to make sure it holds air pressure. Without a spare, if you get a flat tire, you will have to unhitch, take the wheel off of the trailer and leave the trailer along the road until you can return with a repaired tire. You may be surprised to return and not find your boat or trailer. Don't take chances…take a spare.

As with many other marine parts, some new trailer boaters may make the mistake of using automotive parts for marine use. Even when replacing boat trailer tires, you must stay with what the trailer manufacturer recommends. Boat trailers should have tires with strong sidewalls. Radial tires were manufactured for automobiles to give an automobile a smoother ride through the turns. Radial tires on a trailer will cause the trailer to rock back and forth and will build up tire heat, shortening their life. Stiff sidewall tires, those made for trailer use, will not only provide more mileage, but also make it a lot easier to pull the trailer.

While we're talking about wheels, it's important to understand how the wheels are attached to the axle. In most cases the wheels are attached to a hub with four or five lug bolts, similar to an automobile wheel. If you just want to remove the wheel and tire you undo the lugs. If you want to remove the wheel with the hub intact you take off the large nut off that is threaded on the end of the spindle. This nut and a cotter pin (that you have to remove first) are usually under a dust cover at the end of the spindle. When the cotter pin, large nut and large washer are removed, the bearing will be exposed. As you slowly pull the wheel toward you the bearing will pop out. The job gets a little more involved if your trailer has brakes. Bearings wear out from not having enough grease, overloading the trailer and using the wrong grease. When you've burnt a bearing on a long trip, you'll soon add a spare bearing or two to your toolbox.

It's really very simple to take care of the wheels on your trailer. Just keep them greased with a good waterproof grease, made for marine applications. Most good trailers have grease fittings already in place on the wheel hubs. That makes it unnecessary to pull the wheels off to pack the bearings with grease. If your trailer does not have grease fittings you can get an adapter kit for most trailers and install the grease fittings yourself. Even if you're not really handy with tools, you can do it. The main thing is to make sure the bearings are greased regularly and checked monthly. Bearing Buddies are a great help in this ritual. When you are packing the wheels with grease, it's a good idea to smear a light coating of grease on the inside of the trailer coupler and hitch ball.

Some trailers used for larger and heavier boats come equipped with brakes. There are two types of break used on trailers, electric or hydraulic surge systems. Electric brakes may be found on trailers used just for towing larger boats, but rarely do manufacturers put electric brakes on trailers that will be submerged in water. Electric brakes are wired to the brake system or brake lights of the tow vehicle. The more popular braking system is the hydraulic surge system that rely on the force created on the trailer when the tow vehicle's brakes are activated. The more the force on the coupler, the harder the surge-activated braking system applies pressure to the brake pads on wheels of the trailer. Trailer boaters will find conventional, as well as disc brakes, on boat trailers. Hydraulic brake systems are constructed so the braking system becomes inactive when the tow vehicle is intentionally putting pressure on the trailer coupler, as when backing up.

Before you take off with your trailer in tow, here's a quick checklist. Starting from the front, check the hitch and make sure the coupler and lock pin are in place. Is the coupler down tight on the ball? Check the safety chains and make sure there is enough play so the chains don't bind in turns. Make sure there is not so much chain that the chain drags on the ground. Walk around the boat and make sure all the tie down straps are tight. Check the wheels and hubs and make sure the tires are properly inflated and have good rubber. Then make a general walk-around inspection to make sure everything seems right. With a little care your boat trailer will be trouble free.

Trailer Boats -- *Alex Zidock, Jr.*

CHAPTER SEVEN
TOWING ABC'S

For some new boaters, and even some "old salts" that never owned a boat trailer, the thought of towing a boat represents another challenge to boating. Many think the ability to tow is an inherent trait that surfaces only in generations whose family tree has nautical branches and a deep-rooted wanderlust. Not so. Trailering a small boat is an easily learned skill. Once accomplished it will open a whole new world of boating fun and adventure.

You may have a hitch already installed on the vehicle you are considering to use towing your boat. If not, some light duty hitches can be installed by boaters handy with tools. It is, however, extremely important to remember the hitch is the link between two valuable vehicles, and it must be able to handle the stress and strain applied when stopping, starting and turning on the way to and from your destination. It's nearly impossible with newer cars, but never attach or attempt to attach a hitch to the bumper of an automobile. Bumpers are not made for that purpose and this improper application will create a very dangerous situation.

The hitch and trailer coupler must be rated to carry the load of boat and trailer. If you want sway-free towing, the hitch must be set at the right height to properly, and safely pull the unit you have in mind. The best bet is to have a boat dealer or other professional check your current hitch, if you have one, before you attach the trailer. Or let them install the proper hitch to match your specific trailer and boat combination.

The dealer can also adjust the position of the boat on the trailer to create the proper tongue weight. Some experts agree heavier loads should carry 10 to 15 percent of the gross weight on the trailer tongue. But, depending on the trailer configuration and size, this figure could be as little as 5 percent. You can easily measure the tongue weight of your trailer/boat combination by placing a bathroom scale under the trailer coupler when the coupler is at its towing height.

Beside the weight of the boat and trailer, you have to take into consideration the weight of the additional gear you will keep on your boat, including the freshwater storage and fuel tanks.

Frequently, people who tow their boats use them as utility trailers and stow luggage, coolers full of food and beverages, and other supplies in their boat for the ride to the launch destination. While this frees up space in the tow vehicle for passengers and other necessities, it ads to the tongue weight and may put unacceptable stress on the trailer frame and tires. Gasoline weighs about 6-pounds per gallon. 100 gallons of gasoline in your boat tank could add 600-pounds to the gross weight of your rig. That's why it's better to gas-up once you've reached your destination.

Advantages: Even if you live at the edge of water and have your own slip, you may want to pull your boat out of the water for maintenance or storage. Completing that task with your own trailer is convenient and saves you money. Also, when you own a trailer you can store your boat on land. The bottom will stay clean, you will save marina fees and it may be safer to store the boat in your own driveway or yard. If your boat is called upon to handle a variety of family recreational duties a trailer is a must. You can haul to new launches, cruise new locations, explore waterside attractions and restaurants, or you can find a quiet cove where water skiing is at its best. If fishing is on the agenda, you have the opportunity to change your venue on any given day.

Backing up: Ask ten people what is their biggest concern about towing a boat and most will say, "backing up." Yet, once the driver understands the relationship of the tow vehicle to the trailer, the exercise becomes nearly automatic. There seems to be two popular methods of controlling the direction of the trailer while going backward. Some drivers put their hand on the top of the steering wheel and use the side-view or rearview mirrors, or they look back over their shoulder and direct the boat where they want it to go. If that's not easy for you, try putting your hand on the bottom of the steering wheel. Now, if the tow vehicle and the trailer are in a straight line, and you're moving backward, whatever direction you move the steering wheel is the direction the trailer will go. Go slow – turn slow! Using either method, once the trailer is going in the direction you want, turn the wheel in the opposite direction to control the degree of turn, and allow the tow vehicle to follow the boat around the turn. This sounds a lot harder than it really is. Remember, when going in reverse, slightly turning the wheel of the tow vehicle will get big results at the trailer. The best place to practice with your new trailer is in an area of a parking lot, free of other vehicles. Take along some empty cardboard boxes and try maneuvering around them, going forward and backward. It's not courteous or safe to practice at the boat launch ramp.

Check list: There have been entire books written about trailering boats. But what stands out are the pages that contain check lists and towing tips. It's a good idea to put your own checklist together and keep a laminated copy of it in the glove compartment of the tow vehicle. Safety should be at the top of everyone's list, so here are a few items to start you off in the right direction.

The Hitch: Inspect the ball on the hitch and make sure the bolt and nut are secure. There should be a lock washer on the bolt between the nut and the hitch tongue of the tow vehicle. If the hitch is bolted onto the tow vehicle, check those bolts regularly, before and during any extended trip. If the hitch is welded, check for cracks in the welds. Do the same check on the tongue of the trailer, examining the coupler and the coupler latch. Each towing ball and each coupler is marked with its size. Do not attempt to tow a trailer if the ball on the tow vehicle hitch and coupler on the trailer are two different sizes. Tow balls start at 1-7/8-inches and increase in size by 1/8-inch increments. There are a variety of hitch combinations on the market, including load-leveler types, that allow easier and safer towing of heavier units.

Safety Chains: Once you have secured the trailer to the tow vehicle attach the safety chains. Most states require that two chains be attached to the trailer and to the tow vehicle. The breaking strength of the chains should be 1-1/2 times the maximum gross trailer weight. Make sure the chains are long enough so they do not bind when going around a turn and short enough so they do not drag on the ground. It is actually better to have the safety chains bolted onto the trailer tongue and looped through the hitch frame by putting a bolt through two links of the chain. Chains that are welded to the trailer are not as strong. Heat from welding weakens the welded link and could cause the chain to break, should the tow vehicle and trailer separate.

Electrical: After you check the wiring harness for dirt and fraying, make the electrical connections. To maintain good electrical contact, connections should be sprayed regularly with a lubricant that displaces moisture. Check all of the lights on the trailer to make sure they work. The first time you connect a trailer to a tow vehicle you may notice the turn signal lights will flash rapidly. The problem is you've placed an extra load on the standard turn signal flasher, which is probably the original equipment on the tow vehicle. Replacement with a heavy-duty flasher is easy, costs only a few dollars and will solve the problem. If other lights won't work, first check the bulbs. If your trailer is the type you can submerge to launch and retrieve your boat, you might have some corrosion on the bulb contacts. Clean with steel wool and then coated with heavy grease to prevent future corrosion problems. If that doesn't work, look for a broken wire between the wiring harness and the lights.

Tires: Most boat trailer tires are replaced, not from tread wear but, because the rubber rots from the sun and weather, and the sidewalls crack from improper inflation. Rule one is always carry a spare tire mounted and locked to the trailer frame. Tires on boat trailers fail when the spare is in the trunk of your tow car and you're using another tow vehicle ...just for one short trip.

Carry your own tire pressure gauge and check for proper inflation frequently. Under inflation is much worse than over inflation. When a tire is under inflated, the flexing of the sidewalls builds heat rapidly which causes the tires to crack, delaminate and blow. Since hot air expands, the proper time to check your tire pressure is before a trip, when the tires are cool. If a tire is rated to contain 25 pounds of air and it is three pounds low when it's cool, it could be just right by the time you drive to a service station. Put the three pounds in anyway. Tire manufacturers allow for tire expansion once they warm up. They'll reach the correct pressure again upon cooling.

Tie Down: You may think because you cannot lift the stern of the boat that the bow eye, where the winch rope or cable is hooked, is enough to keep the boat on the trailer when underway. You may think the weight of the boat alone will hold the boat securely on the trailer even for a short drive. Wrong. This is an extremely dangerous practice. Beside the bow hook, most new boats have transom straps that ratchet tight and then snap closed holding the boat tightly against the trailer. Many boats have gunwale straps that provide more security. Use them both! Check these straps for wear whenever you prepare to tow your boat.

Odds & Ends: Beside those things we do for safety reasons when we tow a boat and trailer, there are hundreds of tips on trailer care and maintenance. Regular maintenance and plain old common sense will add years to the life of any boat and trailer.

If you use your trailer in or near salt water, it will require more care then one that only sees freshwater. The trailer should be hosed off immediately after each exposure to salt water to prevent rust and corrosion, the worst enemies of boat trailers. Wheel lugs should be checked frequently on all trailers but lugs exposed to salt water should be removed at least once a year and coated with an anti-seize compound. To keep trailer springs in good condition they should be coated with a mixture of equal parts of heavy oil and mineral spirits at least once a year. Wheel bearings should be packed with grease at least once a year or the wheel hubs should be fitted with Bearing Buddies, devices that keep the bearings greased while keeping water out.

Look around you as you travel the highways and you'll see thousands of onetime novice boaters towing their boats with ease and confidence. They learned as you will, the more you practice the better you get. The better you get, the more pleasure you'll get from your trailerable boat.

Trailer Boats -- Alex Zidock, Jr.

Trailer Boats -- *Alex Zidock, Jr.*

CHAPTER EIGHT
TOW VEHICLES

Before you go shopping for a trailerable boat you must decide if your current vehicle is up to the job of towing a boat and what size boat it can tow. If the vehicle is a newer automobile it may not be rated to tow anything, let alone a boat. If you think you can modify your new car to tow a boat, you better read your owner's manual. Pay strict attention to what is covered in the warranty and how the warranty can be voided by the manufacturer because of your modifications. Older cars were not always the best tow vehicles, but the larger ones offered more tolerances just because of their bulkier construction. Today's automobile drive trains and suspensions are not up to the towing task either. Fortunately, more and more people are buying heavy duty vehicles like pickup trucks, vans and Sport Utility Vehicles (SUV) which are built to handle loads. They all make good tow vehicles but you need to match the size of the tow vehicle with the size of the job you expect it to do.

Manufacturers of most vehicles have rated their vehicles as to its towing capacity. You will find in the owners manual, or possibly on the inside of a door, the Gross Vehicle Weight Rating (GVWR), which is the maximum weight supported on the axles of the vehicle. Another measurement is the Gross Combined Weight Rating (GCWR), which is the total weight of the tow vehicle and whatever is being towed, combined. You also may find in your tow vehicle owner's manual, the Trailer Weight Allowance (TWA). You need to understand these terms and what they mean before you buy a boat.

The GVWR takes into consideration the actual weight of the vehicle and then allows for passengers, fuel, gear and anything else you may want to put in or on the vehicle. If you load the vehicle with people, supplies, coolers of food and other needs, and that brings the GVWR up to the maximum recommended by the manufacturer, you better stop. If you proceed to hang a boat trailer with an additional 150-pound hitch weight onto it, you could be asking for trouble.

The GCWR is the weight of the tow vehicle, including the passengers, fuel and other items you packed into the vehicle. Add the weight of the boat, motor, trailer, and the fuel in the boat, and all other accessories and anything else you pile in the boat for the ride to the water. Remember, gasoline weighs about 6 pound per gallon and water is about one pound heavier. The TWA is the total weight the manufacturer has determined your tow vehicle can pull.

If you already own a vehicle you think is rated for towing, just stop by your local garage or dealership and ask their opinion. They may suggest you install some add-ons to help your tow vehicle cope with the added strains of towing a boat.

As an example, they may suggest beefing up the suspension, adding an additional unit to your cooling system or even adding oil-cooling units.

If you are going to buy a new vehicle, insist on the best tow package you can afford. Most new trucks come with tow packages but don't buy a small or mid-sized tow vehicle to handle a big boat. It's always preferable to have more muscle in the tow vehicle than you think you'll need.

Don't overlook the need for four wheel or all-wheel drive (AWD) in your tow vehicle. There's nothing more embarrassing than to sit at the bottom of a boat ramp spinning your wheels while going further back down the ramp because rear wheels can't get a grip. Front wheel drive units are less effective since the weight of the boat and trailer and the uphill position of the tow vehicle causes the front end to lift and lose traction. A growing favorite among trailer boaters is the tow vehicles with AWD.

An important part of the tow vehicle is the trailer hitch. After all, this is the only connection you have between the tow vehicle and the boat. Trailer hitches, like tow vehicles, are rated by their manufacturers, so you have a better idea of which hitch for which job.

Starting from the lightweight ones, Class 1 hitches are used only for loads under 2000 pounds. While some Class 1 hitches are made to be fastened to the vehicles rear bumper, this is inadvisable. Older cars had strong bumpers, but today's cars bumpers are not as strong. Class 1 hitches can often be bolted or welded to the vehicles frame, but again, make sure the hitch will do the job. Class 2 hitches are rated up to 3500 pounds. They are permanently fastened or welded to the vehicle's frame. Class 3 hitches are rated for 5,000 pounds and Class 4 hitches can handle up to 10,000 pounds. There is a Class 5 hitch but it is saved for the heaviest towing and is usually fastened to a heavy truck.

The problems that occur with very heavy loads are the tongue weight increases so much the back end of the tow vehicle and the front end of the trailer will dip down. This is an unsafe condition and will cause the trailer to sway when being towed. In this case, a load-equalizing hitch will redistribute the weight so the tow vehicle and the trailer are straight.

Many years ago I had a situation where I stored

Trailer Boats -- *Alex Zidock, Jr.*

my rather heavy wooden boat in my yard and only towed it a dozen or so miles to the marina where I docked it most of the season. Even though it was a short tow, it was difficult because of the heavy tongue weight on my Chevrolet station wagon. When I purchased a travel trailer and a load-equalizing hitch, I couldn't believe how much easier it was to tow.

CHAPTER NINE
LAUNCHING & RETRIEVING

It's one thing to slide behind the wheel of your tow vehicle and head out of the boat dealer's parking lot with your new toy in tow for the first time. It's another thing to get to the water and launch your new boat without a problem, the first time you try. While it's not that difficult, it does take some practice. It's not something you should do on a Fourth of July weekend.

The best place to start learning how to launch your boat is in a large empty parking lot. Take your rig, your imagination and the persons that will be with you when you will be using the boat. You'll also need four to six pylons or cardboard boxes. Place two boxes on each side of your imaginary 'ramp' and one or two boxes at the 'water's edge.' Besides knowing how to back the trailer down the launch ramp and into the water, there's some launch etiquette to be considered.

First of all you're coming to the launch area. Most launch areas have 'staging' or preparation-to-launch areas where certain pre-launch procedures are completed before you even approach the ramp itself. You do these pre-launch duties in the staging area so you don't tie up the ramp area.

Stop the vehicle in the pre-launch area. Make sure the tow vehicle shift lever is placed in park and the emergency brake is on. In gear for manual transmissions.

When you exit the tow vehicle, make sure you close the doors. Other people approaching the launch ramp should be able to get around you. Depending on the size and style of your trailerable boat, you may have to remove the cover to get to the drain plug. Find and insert the drain plug in the transom of the boat. While you're in the parking lot consider, a method that will make the drain plug automatic in your mind. Make sure you store the plug in the same place or better yet, attached it with a light chain near the drain hole. It may seem silly, but every season I see at least one boat launched and nearly sunk because the captain forgot to insert the drain plug.

Proceed to remove the rest of the boat cover and stow it out of the way. At this point, before you begin to load the boat with coolers, skis and other personal gear, check the gear that stays aboard the boat all of the time. If life jackets are stored in lockers, make sure the lockers are unlocked and the jackets are accessible. Check other safety equipment such as fire extinguishers, anchors and lines. Disconnect the electrical harness between the tow vehicle and the trailer. Moving the vehicle around and backing down the ramp the bulbs may get hot and pop when they get introduced to the cool water.

When you begin to unload your boat, be sure whatever you bring aboard it is placed in a way so the boat will remain balanced. Keep in mind how many passengers you're going to have, and where they will sit. Put the wheel chocks in an easy place so they are ready when you get to the launch.

Check to make sure all of your handling lines are securely fastened to the bow and the stern. Remove the tie downs that hold the boat to the trailer and stow those. Hang the fenders and make sure the outboard motor or sterndrive unit is tilted up but unlocked.

While I've covered some of the basic procedures to pre-launch there may be some other things you'll want to do depending on the size of your boat and the activities you have planned. What is important at pre-launch is you have a regular routine. Because there is usually so much activity and excitement just before its time to go boating, some captains have laminated checklists they use for pre-launch.

The next step is important too. Since you have not been out on the water yet, you need to be aware of the conditions before you approach the launch ramp. While you're still in the parking lot, take the time to walk around your rig, checking as you go to make sure you're ready for launch and everything is still okay. Now walk over to the 'ramp' and watch another boat being launched. Try and determine if that launcher had trouble with the current, the wind or the water depth. Is the ramp slippery? Which way is the wind blowing? Is the water high or low?

If this is your first time at the ramp you may even want to watch another boater go through an entire launch procedure. Don't schedule your first day at the ramp during a weekend.

When you're ready to launch your boat, make sure you have not left anything behind at the pre-launch area. Children and pets must be taken under tow and kept in a safe area until the boat is successfully launched and secured to the dock. You and other boaters will be trying to complete an operation you don't do everyday. It takes a lot of concentration, which makes it difficult to watch for kids and pets. Before you enter the tow vehicle, check once again that the drain plug has been inserted and locked properly.

If there is room at the launch ramp, you want to pull the boat to the ramp and turn as sharply away from the ramp as you can so the tow vehicle and the boat are in a straight line with the ramp. It is helpful to have another person watching and guiding you while you are backing up to the ramp. Back down the ramp until the trailer tires are touching the water. In the parking lot, you can back up until you bump the cardboard boxes you've set as guides. Stop the tow vehicle, set the brakes and place the chocks behind the wheels of the tow vehicle

Now you can't go any further in your practice session in the parking lot. But, if you've mastered the procedure so far, you'll be pretty well prepared when you do get to the actual launch ramp. For practice, while you are in the empty parking lot, drive around and get the feel of the relationship between the tow vehicle and the trailer. Try parallel parking and for a real test, see if you can accomplish a 'K' turn. Just remember to practice these maneuvers slowly. Don't forget when you are backing up, a slight turn of the steering wheel makes a big difference in trailer movement.

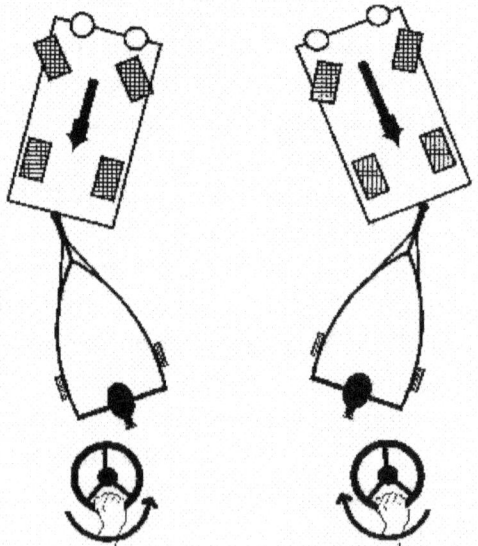

Figure 11
Backing a trailer will be easy if you follow this diagram.

When you are ready for the real thing, here's how to proceed once you have the trailer on the ramp and wheels chocked. Have someone hold the bow line and the stern line from the launch ramp or the dock.

If your trailer is the tilt type, release the tilt latch and then release the anti-reverse lock on the winch. With the cable still attached to the bow eye, slowly allow the boat to slide off the trailer while you maintain control with the winch lever. Attach the dock lines to the dock or have someone hold them. Unhook the winch cable and rewind it back into the winch. Some winch cables are metal and the launcher must be careful not to grab the cable where frayed strands may cause injury to the hands.

This procedure works well with trailers that have rollers. If you have a bunk-type trailer, you may have to back the trailer further into the water to float the boat off the bunks. How far you put the trailer into the water depends on several things. One thing for sure, never back your rig up so far that the rear wheels of the tow vehicle are in the water. Backing too far will submerge the exhaust pipe and stall the tow vehicle. Then you may need a tow to get the tow vehicle and the trailer out of the water and back up the ramp.

Once the boat is floating, help the person who is holding the lines secure the boat to the dock. Then return to the trailer and tilt it back to its normal position (if it's the tilt type) and lock it in place. Remove the chocks and slowly drive the tow vehicle and trailer to the parking area.

While you don't want to waste time during your entire launch procedure, you should not hurry either. It's a matter of getting accustom to what must be done and doing it as part of a routine. The more you do it, the easier it becomes, and the more enjoyment it adds to boating.

Once you return to the boat, you need to lower the outboard or sterndrive, connect fuel lines and follow the normal procedure for starting the engine. While the engine is warming up, load any remaining gear, passengers and pets. Make sure everyone knows where the life jackets are stowed and everyone has a seat before you cast off. Move away from the launch area very slowly and watch for other boats coming into the area. Secure lines and bumpers before you increase your speed.

BACK ON THE TRAILER

After a fun day on the water you'll want to put your boat back on the trailer for the ride home. Preparation for hauling out begins before you reach the launch area. Start by making sure all of the personal things you and your guests have brought on board are secured and out of the way. Approach the launch area very slowly and allow any other boater the same courtesy you would expect. If there is a dock next to the launch ramp, set out your bumpers, pull up to the dock and fasten the bow and stern lines. Unload your passengers and any personal items they might want to take with them. Remember, you will have time to take out skis and coolers once you have the boat on the trailer and out of the way of other boaters who want to launch or retrieve their boats.

Once the boat is unloaded, return with the trailer, backing the trailer down the launch ramp. Put the chocks under the tow vehicle wheels. If it is the roller type trailer that tilts, guide the boat onto the rollers and fasten the winch cable to the bow eye. Using the bow and stern lines, have your helper keep the boat straight while you crank the winch, pulling the boat onto the trailer. Be aware the boat should retrieve easily and too much strain on the winch cable could cause it to snap.

If your trailer is the bunk type, position the trailer in the water and repeat the same process. Some trailers are made so the boat can actually be driven on, at least part way, using the boat motor. This is a practice done only by experienced boaters who know how to handle this operation and who know the water at the launch ramp is deep enough so the propeller won't hit the bottom.

Once the boat is positioned all the way, and straight, on the trailer use a tie down or two to hold the boat in place while you pull the trailer up the launch ramp. Remove the wheel chocks. Once you have the boat up the ramp and out of the way, you can take more time to secure it with more tie downs.

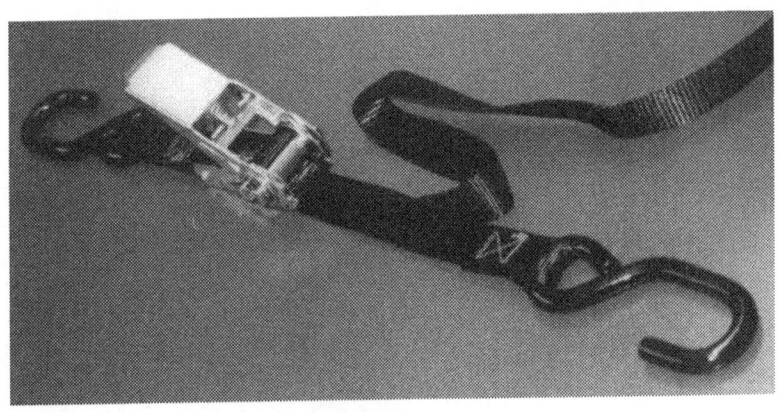

Figure 12
Courtesy of the manufacturer.

Typical ratchet tie-down.

Pull the drain plug and if it is not fastened, stow it where you will find it the next time you launch. Your boat and trailer needs a freshwater bath as soon as possible. All brightwork should be cleaned and dried. During the wipe-down process is a good time to inspect the boat for any damage that may have occurred during use. Check the propeller(s) for nicks, the gelcoat for gouges and made sure cleats are still tight. Disconnect fuel lines if needed, secure all gear, cover the boat and while you are reconnecting the trailer's electrical harness, make one final inspection of the trailer and tow hitch. You're ready for the road.

CHAPTER TEN
HELMSMANSHIP & SEAMANSHIP

If you do most of your boating on the big water, big rivers, bays and the ocean, you probably have a better understanding what helmsmanship is all about. I'm sure you have stood in awe while a larger boat seemed to glide effortless into a tight docking space. Maneuvering a boat with finesse is not luck, it's a practiced art that comes with experience, and a certain feel a good boat captain gets when he knows his equipment, the boats characteristics and her limitations. Helmsmanship is probably best described as the part YOU play in making your boat do what you want her to do, and understanding why she does it.

Several years ago I had a 30-foot overnighter with a flybridge over a large cabin and a single screw. She taught me a lot about boat handling. I would not have been as comfortable learning had I not gotten my primary education knocking around in car-toppers, canoes and runabouts for 20 previous years. When I first began to run *Another Story*, and I would get into a tight situation (If I would have to back down into a slip in sloppy weather with the wind blowing in one direction and the tide going in another), I'd always try to simplify the situation. I mentally put myself back into the 18-foot Grumman Fish & Ski I used to own, and consider what I had to do to make the bigger boat do what I wanted her to do. The more I ran the big boat, the more familiar she became, and soon I could handle most maneuvering situations with ease.

The one thing I learned very quickly was the effect the wind had on a high boat as opposed to a powerboat that sat close to the water. A raised cabin and superstructure above acts like a sail. You soon understand why a slight breeze can move a sailboat along at a good clip.

While a lot of practice makes you a good boat handler, it really helps if you have some general idea how to do things the nautical way. While I'm talking about helmsmanship and how to handle a boat, I'm also going to discuss a little about seamanship. Seamanship may best be described as the understanding of nautical procedure, boat equipment and how it all works

If you have not done so, and you own or are contemplating a boat, you should take a safe boating course. There are a several good reasons. One, your insurance costs less. Boats and boating etiquette are, for the most part, foreign to most people who don't own boats, and the course will give you a safety advantage. People read manuals, study the rules and regulations, and then must pass a driving test to operate an automobile. People need only to have enough money to buy a boat, register it, and without any education, can operate it. (Except for personal watercraft where certain restrictions apply in some states). If you spend sufficient time on the water, you've met the ones who have no nautical education. Like the boater who needs a tow but only has short dock lines on board. Or the one who throws his anchor overboard without first fastening the other end to something. Or the boater who pulls up to the stern of a trolling fisherman to ask if he's catching anything.

To get a better idea of helmsmanship and seamanship is all about let's explore some topics by way of taking a quiz first.

1. You're traveling at a safe speed and another boater pulls up behind you and toots his horn. What do you think he wants? What do you do?
2. Same situation except the boat is coming right at you and he toots his horn. What does it mean?
3. You come out of a waterside restaurant where your boat is tied parallel to the dock. Now there is a boat in front of you and one in back of you on the dock. How do you get away from the dock?
4. It's night and you see a boat crossing in front of you. If you both continue on course there will be a collision. What action do you take?
5. You're headed to your favorite fishing hole and you notice a boat with the American flag flying up side down. Does that mean the fish aren't biting?

You are in your car and you're on the way to a favorite launch ramp and all of a sudden someone pulls out in front of you. You're forced to slam on your brakes so hard you think your boat is going to slide off the trailer right up and over your tow vehicle. You blast your horn at least three times at the jerk. That may be acceptable driving etiquette on land. But if someone does something stupid when you're on the water and you blast your horn three times, it simply means you're going to put your boat in reverse.

Horn signals. Not too may boaters even know they exist. If you are running your boat and another boat pulls up behind you and gives you one blast from his horn, it's not a social "Hi, there," it means he or she is going to turn to starboard and pass you on his port side. The passing boater knows you know what he is going to do, you are supposed to respond by giving him one blast back and maintain your speed and course. If he comes up on your stern and gives you two short horn blasts, it means he is going to turn to port and pass you on your port side.

If another boat is coming at you, bow to bow, and you give him one blast, it means you intend to move starboard and you will pass each other port to port. The other boat should respond with one blast and move to his starboard for a safe pass. There are other horn signals boaters should also know.

Figure 13
Courtesy of the manufacturer.

Typical flush mounted horn.

What's starboard and port anyway? Here's an easy way to remember port and starboard. Use the phrase, "Johnny LEFT PORT with a RED nose." This tells you, as you are sitting in your boat facing toward the bow, (pointy end) the port side is on your left side. That leaves the right side to be the starboard side.

This little saying has a tie to the buoy system in the United States too. If you boat on navigable waterways, ones that have marker buoys, you will remember as you LEAVE PORT or head downstream, that all of the RED buoys will be on your LEFT side. Some of the safe boating classes teach the three R's, RED, RIGHT, RETURN. This means that when you are coming from the ocean or from down stream to a port up stream, the RED buoys will be on your RIGHT when you RETURN. If you took a safe boating course, you would know one side of the channel is marked with red nun buoys or red triangular day marks and on the other side of the channel the buoys are green cans or green square day marks. What help is this to you? It is easy to get lost or turned around on the water at night or in a fog. If you are on a waterway that has buoys, you can at least tell if you are going upstream or downstream and what side of the channel you are on.

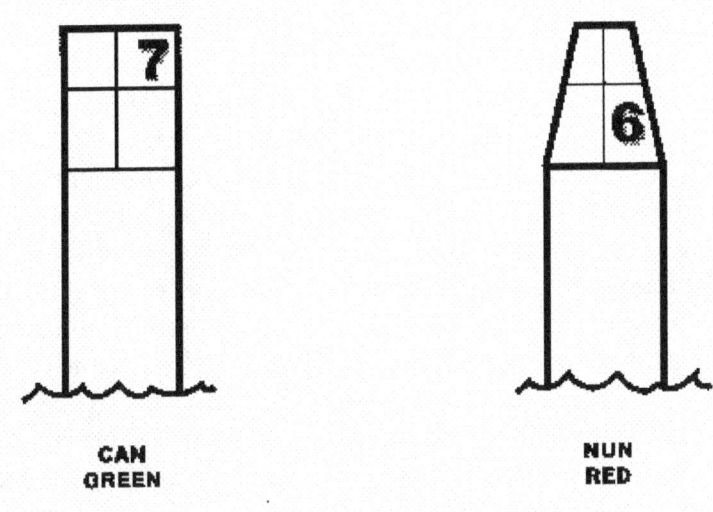

Figure 14
Two of the most common channel markers.

One of the most interesting areas to explore when we talk about helmsmanship and seamanship is the use of lines. There are no ropes aboard a vessel. You go into a store and select rope for your boat, but once you bring the cordage aboard the boat it becomes a line. In the olden days of big sailing ships, line was made from hemp and manila. Modern lines are stronger, more abrasion resistant and easier on the hands. Most lines are made of synthetics, like nylon, polyester and polypropylene. The latter is usually the weakest and least expensive.

Lines are used for many purposes. Different parts of the line are called different things. The end you are working, usually the one you hold and are tying to something is called the bitter end. The middle of a line is the bight, which is also the part of the line you would use to make loops and knots.

In most cases boaters are familiar with the line attached to an anchor. The anchor line is called the rode. Some other lines are familiar even to novice boaters. You use the bow line and the stern line to tie the boat to the dock or piling. For seasoned boaters the spring line is probably the most useful. Particularly when you come out of a restaurant and your boat has been boxed in at the dock. By casting off the stern line and the bow line, you can use a spring line to either move the bow or the stern straight away from the dock to maneuver out of the tight situation. The spring line can also be used in reverse to get the boat into a tight docking spot with the same ease.

O.K. It doesn't look easy on paper but believe me, with a little practice you can do it. Of course, the best place to practice any maneuver is at a dock that does not have other boats around.

I live on Lake Wallenpaupack in the Pennsylvania Pocono Mountains and there's little that can compare to getting out on the lake just before dark, in the middle of the summer when the smallies are hitting top water lures. But this is a midweek deal only. Anyone who knows anything about the lake knows that you keep the boat at the dock Friday and Saturday nights, when the lake becomes a zoo. The big lake attracts a lot of boaters and many of them have no idea there are such things as "Rules of the Road" that apply to boating. Helmsmanship, seamanship and common sense are not usually spoken here during the weekends. During the week, when there is a lot less boat traffic, it's a boater's paradise.

Whether I am boating on my home lake or any other lake in the United States, I always proceed with caution, even when I know I have the right of way. At night, if I see a boat crossing in front of me from left to right showing me his green light, I don't assume he knows I am the stand-on vessel and he is the give-way vessel. I know if a boat is crossing my bow from right to left, he is the vessel that has the right of way and I have to adjust my course to avoid a collision. In either case, I proceed with caution and expect the other vessel to do the unexpected. Fortunately, with more and more people taking basic boating courses, more and more people are beginning to understand what the lights on boats mean. The one rule that applies to all boating, is every boater has the responsibility to avoid a collision with another boat at any cost.

Regardless of who has the right of way, it boils down to one simple to remember term; "The Law Of Gross Tonnage." In other words, "In a collision at sea, he with the biggest boat wins."

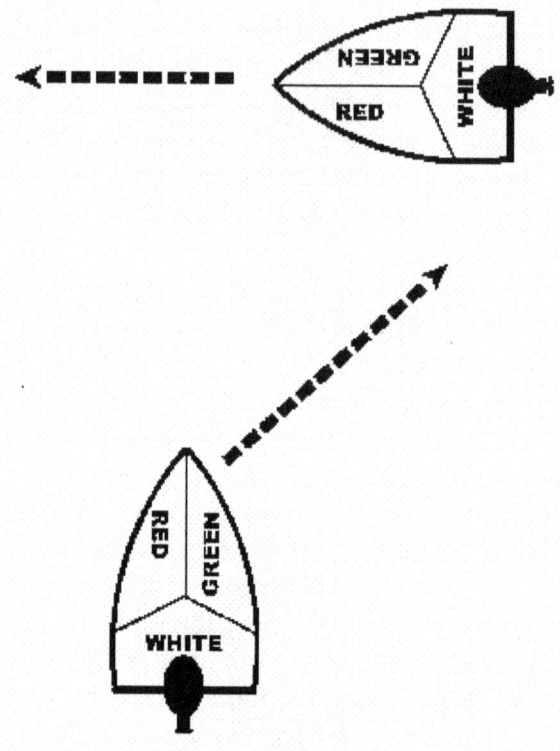

Figure 15

Crossing situation and the visible lights.

I would think every boater would want to take a safe boating course just to learn what to do in case of an emergency. Being in a boat is not like being on land in an automobile where you can just get out and walk if you experience a problem.

Most trailerable boats registered in the U.S., particularly those used primarily on inland waters, are not equipped with marine (VHF) radios. Granted the advent of the cell phone has made communication with shore easier, but how can you get the attention of another boater if you have an emergency or if you just run out of gas. There are several ways and one of them is to fly a flag up side down. Depending on where you boat, and the size and type of your boat, you may be required to carry Coast Guard approved flares or smoke devices. If you use flares make sure the flares are the proper ones and they are still in date. If not, they are unacceptable if the marine police stop you.

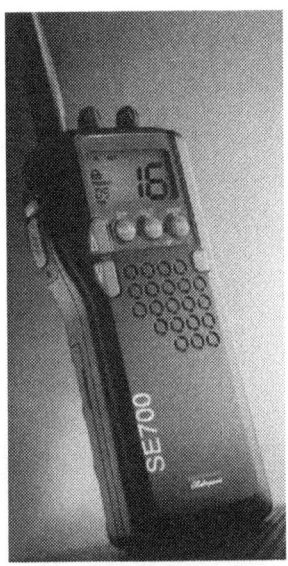

Figure 15a
Courtesy of the manufacturer.

A portable VHF radio can be easily stowed on any boat.

The good thing about learning helmsmanship and seamanship is you only need to learn enough to satisfy your immediate boating circumstance, or if you want, you can learn a lot more depending on your interest. Marlinespike seamanship, as example is a great hobby that pays off on land as well as on the water. It's the part of boating that deals with learning how to splice lines and tie knots. Entire books have been written on the subject.

Boating becomes more fun, as you become more proficient in completing basic tasks. Learning to become a better helmsman, studying seamanship and taking more interest in doing things correctly on the water, offers you and your passengers the edge on safety afloat.

Trailer Boats -- *Alex Zidock, Jr.*

CHAPTER ELEVEN
ALL ABOUT GASOLINE

Few people realize when they pull up to a gasoline pump they may experience more than a change in the way their gasoline smells. There are certain things about today's gasoline every boater should know. Some of these properties could cause a change in the performance of your automobile, light truck, ATV or boat engine. There is reason for concern about the new gasoline available in today's marketplace.

Besides meeting certain standards, as set by state and federal regulations, refineries blend their gasoline in accordance with specifications set by the American Society for Testing and Materials (ASTM). The combined input from ASTM members, which is made up of representatives from the automobile industry, boat and other engine manufacturing companies, gasoline producers and pipeline companies, has lead to the development of the specifications to which all refiners must finish their basic gasoline product to ensure minimal quality standards. It is only then, gasoline manufacturers can proceed to customize their brand with detergents, antiknock compounds and other additives.

Gasoline, in its simplest form, is a complex mixture of hydrocarbons, which are molecules that contain hydrogen and carbon, and are refined from crude oil. The hydrocarbons are blended with more than 150 chemicals into a volatile fuel used to make internal combustion engines work.

Trailer Boats -- *Alex Zidock, Jr.*

To enhance gasoline, manufacturers introduce any number of additives. These include antioxidants and metal deactivators which slow down gum formation and improve the stability, deposit modifiers to reduce spark plug pre-ignition and fouling, surfactants and freezing point depressants to improve vaporization, prevent icing and reduce objective emissions, corrosion inhibitors, which prevent gasoline from corroding storage tanks and dyes to color the product for safety and regulatory purposes. Other important additives are the octane-enhancing compounds used to improve octane ratings.

Manufacturers of gasoline change their blends to keep up with engine technology and EPA regulations. In the 1980s, when fuel injection systems were introduced, there were significant problems with deposits accumulating on intake valve surfaces. Additives were introduced into gasoline blends to keep valves and injectors clean. In some instances, however, certain additives may only be added to higher octane grades of gasoline. Since there are no regulations governing which additives can be introduced in which grades, some gasoline will burn better in certain engines. If your boat, ATV or other gas-powered vehicle is properly tuned and in good condition, but runs poorly while using the correct octane gasoline recommended for that engine, you may improve performance just by switching to another brand of fuel with the same octane rating. Boats that are permanently moored at a marina may have more difficulty managing this. Boaters who trailer their boat have the advantage of stopping almost anywhere for fuel.

Gasoline is measured on an Antiknock Index or octane, which is a way of determining the gasoline's ability to resist pre-ignition, or engine knock. The Antiknock Index is listed at the pump as 87 octane, 89 octane and so on. Occasionally you'll see a sticker on the gas pump that reads (R+M)/2 Method. The R is the

Research Octane Number, which is the gasoline's ability to resist knock at low speed and under no strain. The M is the Motor Octane Number, which is the fuel's ability to resist knock at high speeds and under a heavy load. By averaging these two numbers, researchers determine an octane rating which defines how well the gasoline will resist engine knock under average conditions.

Engine knock is an important factor to consider to maintain performance, and enjoy longevity from any gasoline, internal combustion engine.

Engine knock is caused by pre-ignition of gasoline as it is compressed inside the cylinder, just milliseconds before the normal spark plug firing. Most drivers notice this when putting a load on their tow vehicle engine, pulling a boat up a steep ramp, or climbing a particularly steep hill and pressing on the accelerator to gain speed. When knock occurs, the vehicle loses power and fuel economy is reduced causing internal damage to the engine.

A wide variety of conditions can promote engine knock: outdoor temperatures, humidity, altitude, placing a heavy load or strain on an engine, the age of the vehicle, and time elapsed between tune-ups. Occasional engine knock can be addressed by using higher octane gasoline. If you are taking your everyday vehicle on vacation, towing a boat or trailer, you may lessen incidences of engine knock by increasing the octane of the gasoline you use. Persistent engine knock will destroy your engine, particularly if your vehicle is an older model. You may try using gasoline with a higher octane rating, but if you cannot stop the knock, you probably need a tune-up.

With the advent of sophisticated, engine management systems on newer automobiles, as well as modern boats, engines can operate efficiently using a variety of fuels of different octane ratings. It is better to use a gasoline that contains the octane rating recommended for your car, light truck or boat motor. The best information to determine which octane gasoline you should use is your owner's manual. Each manufacturer will list the minimum octane to use, under average conditions. Using a lessor octane fuel than recommended will cause problems. Incorrectly burned fuel builds layers of carbon deposits on cylinder walls, exhaust ports, spark plugs and piston ring grooves.

Once you have found the correct brand of fuel and octane rating for an engine, stick with it. Using fuel with a higher octane will not give the engine more power, or give it better fuel economy. The engine will already be operating at optimum settings and the higher octane will have no effect on the engine management system. If you are currently using a fuel with less octane than your engine requires, you may be able to enjoy an increase in power and fuel economy by using a higher octane fuel, which would move the engine management system to perform at its optimum settings.

Nearly a decade ago Congress passed a set of amendments to the Clean Air Act of 1967. This addressed cleaner burning gasoline and resulted in refineries adding oxygenates to gasoline to reduce the reactivity of emissions. Most oxygenates contain alcohol or ethers. Methyl tertiary-butyl ether (MTBE) and ethyl alcohol (ethanol) have been the oxygenates most commonly used in gasoline. These new gasolines became known as oxygenated gasoline. In 1995 the hydrocarbon structure of these new fuels was so significantly modified, these gasolines became known as the cleaner burning, or reformulated gasolines (RFG).

The use of oxygenated, or reformulated gasolines, is not widespread, but it has been required in some major metropolitan areas of the United States, and in all of California, during the four winter months. Boaters who trailer may be confronted with RFG, and while these new gasolines have contributed to cleaner air by burning more completely, they have a downside.

RFG users will notice 2 to 3% lower fuel economy than with non-oxygenated gasolines. By increasing oxygen in gasoline the amount of energy in each gallon is reduced, which could reduce mileage by as much as 2 to 3%. RFG costs a few cents a gallon more than non-oxygenated gasoline. In engines more than ten years old, RFG could produce a fire hazard. This factor is very important for owners of older outboard and inboard boat engines.

Natural and synthetic rubbers used in hoses and O-rings, called elastomers, which were in use before RFG and oxygenated gasolines were used, could be affected. Shrinking, swelling, or weakening of these hoses and seals could cause fuel leaks. Because gasoline is highly flammable, there is great risk of fire. RFG may cause even more problems for boaters, since gasoline oxygenated with ethanol attracts moisture. When enough moisture is present, the fuel will separate into two layers, an upper layer of gasoline, and a lower layer of ethanol and water. The lower layer has the potential to corrode fuel system parts. Gasoline oxygenated with MTBE is not susceptible to this problem. In the more current models of outboard motors and inboard engines hoses and O-rings are made of materials not affected by the new gasolines, but check your owner's manual for further information.

Long-term storage becomes more of a problem with oxygenated and reformulated gasolines. The lighter, oxygen-rich hydrocarbons evaporate more readily, and leave molecules that are gummier than when nonoxygenated fuel evaporates. These heavy molecules block fuel filters and carburetor jets. This happens a lot faster in oxygenated or RFG fuel. Boaters who live in areas where there is a drastic climate change and must store their boats during winter months, must top off the tank and add fuel stabilizer to the fuel if the boat will be stored more than 90 days.

The composition of gasoline has undergone tremendous change in the last ten years. Change will continue, as refiners maintain stride with technology, and more EPA regulations take effect in the coming years. Take-it-for-granted gasoline is history. Using only fresh gasoline is the future.

Trailer Boats -- Alex Zidock, Jr.

CHAPTER TWELVE
ALL ABOUT ENGINE OIL

The oil you pour into your four-stroke boat engine does a multitude of things. Much like the human circulatory system, it passes through little tubes and big pipes, maintains certain pressures for certain applications, travels through valves and passages and carries harmful waste and deposits away to be filtered. This lifeblood is kept clean of impurities, and if its flow is not restricted, will contribute to long engine life.

Modern automotive-type engine oil is better than its older cousin. Today's engine oils do not break down or fatigue as quickly under extreme use. This is important especially for marine applications, since marine engines receive more punishment than automobile engines. To match motor oil with a specific task, manufacturers of marine oils have developed a wide variety of formulas. There are oils for 2-cycle outboard engines, oils for 4-stroke outboards and oils for larger I/O's and inboards, blended to provide the best protection for a particular application.

Every manufacturer of marine engines markets oil they claim to be best suited for their product. While some engine manufacturers suggest you must use their engine oils and lubricants to maintain warranties on their products, the Magnuson-Moss Warranty Improvement Act (MMWIA), and general principles of the Federal Trade Commission (FTC) says differently. The act enforces that an engine manufacturer may not make its warranties conditional on the use of any specific brand of motor oil or related lubricants, unless the manufacturer provides such products free of charge. However, if you have an engine still under warranty, it's best to check the fine print. An equipment manufacturer can obtain a waiver of the MMWIA's ruling, only if it provides to the FTC, that the equipment would function properly only if specific brands of motor oil or related lubricants are used.

Motor oil's main job is to lubricate. It keeps your engine from rusting, and actually acts as a sealant between the cylinder walls and the piston rings. It suppresses exhaust and keeps raw gasoline from entering the oil pan or sump, while it coats the cylinder wall with a film of oil, so the rings never, actually, touch the metal of the cylinder walls. In other areas of the engine, motor oil minimizes wear at metal to metal contact. It's a big job, and that's why engine oils have to meet certain standards.

Engine oils, whether used for four-stroke marine application or for automobiles are measured by the Society of Automotive Engineers (SAE), and the information is printed or stamped on every container. The oil is tested at two temperatures. Oils tested at 0°F are marked with a grade number first followed by a "W". The lower the number the thinner the oil. A 5W oil is thin oil and is, usually, used in colder temperatures. Multi use or multigrade oils are also tested at 210°F, the normal operating range for modern engines. These oils are marked with a grade at 0°F first, followed by the letter W and then when the oil heats to 210°, the viscosity rating of the oil. An example might be 5W30 oil. It starts at 5 grade and reaches 30 grade at operating temperature. Viscosity is a measurement of an oils flow characteristics, or thickness, at certain temperatures.

Engine manufacturers have determined which is

the best oil to use with your marine rig and you should stick with it. In many cases, your operator's manual will give you options for cold weather, as well as warm weather operation.

Another emblem you will find on containers of oil meant for four-cycle use, is the circular symbol for the American Petroleum Institute (API). The top half of the donut describes the oil performance levels. The letters SJ is the current designation for gasoline engines. SJ was introduced in 1996 by the SAE. Some older engines may call for oils with the designation of SH or SG. For gasoline engines, however, the highest performance category of oil (SJ) includes the performance properties of each earlier category. If you use oils with the designation SJ in any four-stroke gasoline, engine you will be providing full protection for that engine.

The diesel engine's API performance levels are marked CH-4. However, the latest performance category usually, but not always, includes the performance properties of an earlier performance category. In this case it's best to go to the owners manual for specific instructions if you run a diesel engine in your boat.

Motor oils blended specifically for marine use in four-stroke applications may not carry the API logo, but will usually refer to the designation somewhere on the container. A popular marine blend says: Meets and exceeds API service requirements for SJ, CF-2, CH-4, with a multifunctional additive that assures Marine Grade oil performance.

The new oils are really concoctions of a variety of materials. While they provide protection longer under more adverse conditions, engine oil should be changed regularly to rid the accumulation of debris the detergents scrub from inside the engine. Inhibitors are added to prevent rust, antifoaming agents keep the oil smooth, and other ingredients are added to keep the oil at a constant, operating viscosity. All of these additives eventually break down and quit working. More reasons for changing oil frequently.

We've been talking about oils used in four stroke outboard marine engines, sterndrives and inboards, typically the same type oil used in automobiles. These engines have a pool of oil in an oil sump, or what's more commonly called the oil pan. The engine is constructed so oil is pumped from the reservoir to wherever it's needed in the engine for lubrication, but never mixed with the gasoline.

There's a big difference in the two-cycle engine, where oil has to be mixed with the gasoline for lubrication of the piston rings and cylinder walls. In certain cases, two-stroke-type oil is mixed directly with the gasoline in a gas can, before it is dumped into the engines fuel tank. In direct injection two-cycle engines with oil injection, the oil is poured into the oil reservoir and the oil injection system, accurately, measures the exact amount of oil dispersed and mixed with the gasoline before the mixture is burned. In the old two-stroke technology, the ratio was to mix the gasoline and oil 25:1. This combination often caused spark plugs to foul, produced smoke and bad fuel economy. More recently outboard engine technology has produced engines that run 50:1, or even 100:1, gasoline/oil mixture, which burns nearly as clean as some four-stroke engines. In fact, new direct injection engines burn nearly all the oil mixed with the gasoline so efficiently, this current technology exceeds the U.S. Environmental Protection Agency (USEPA) 2006 standard for two-stroke outboard engines.

Two-cycle engine oil, approved for marine use is certified by the National Marine Manufacturers Association (NMMA), with designations printed on every container. Lubricating oils certified for two-cycle outboards are designated TCW3, and should be used to provide the proper protection for these engines. You'll also find the words, Certified NMMA on the containers of two-stroke marine oils. Regular, automotive-type SJ oil should never be mixed with gasoline and used in two-stroke engines as fuel.

In the beginning of this chapter, I likened engine oil to the human circulatory system. Engine oil, the type used in four-cycle engines, can also be tested to determine what's going on internally in the engine. This could be very important, particularly if you plan a big investment in a used boat that has an I/O or inboard engine.

Oil testing is relatively inexpensive. A $25 analysis could forecast major engine problems. As an example, if water or antifreeze shows up in the oil, one might suspect a problem with a head gasket, or even a cracked head. Since the engine itself is made up of a variety of types of metals, finding an abnormal amount of shavings of certain metals can assume wear in those areas. This does not mean finding small amounts of metals in the oil analysis is bad. Engines wear and one job of the motor oil is to carry impurities, debris and corrosion to the oil filter.

If you pull the dipstick and find the oil is black, that's not bad. Black oil, in fact, means it's doing its job carrying away impurities. If the oil smells like gasoline you may have a problem with piston rings or cylinders. If the oil is milky in color, it means water is getting into your oil. If you notice the last two symptoms, don't start the engine, because you're only going to go for a very short ride. Get the boat to a service technician.

When you change the oil in your boat, take precaution not to dump oil in the boat's bilge. With today's automatic bilge pumps, the accumulated mixture of oil, water and other sludge gather in the darkest depths of your boat. This could easily be dumped overboard without you knowing and cause damage to the water quality of the area. It is also illegal, and you could be fined and forced to pay for the clean up. The use of a crankcase suction pump allows you to suck used oil out of the dipstick and into a 5-gallon bucket. Run the engine until the oil heats up, shut the engine off and drain the oil with the suction pump. This is a good method for routine oil changes in four-cycle boats. However, once a season, the crankcase drain plug should be opened so the oil will carry sediment from the pan.

When you change the oil, it's a good practice to change the filter. Take the same precautions when removing the old filter so excess oil does not escape.

The way in which we boat is changing rapidly. The EPA is seeing to it that marine engine manufacturers meet certain benchmarks in the next several years, to reduce pollution caused by old, outboard motor technology. The new technology in marine propulsion, includes direct-injection, oil-injection, two stroke and four-stroke engines, for both outboard engines and personal watercraft. According to the NMMA, these new technologies offer reduced hydrocarbon exhaust emissions by 80 percent, as compared with conventional two-stoke engines.

Be prepared to move up to the new technology in outboard and four stroke marine engines. Also, be prepared to do regular oil maintenance checks if you want to keep your investment running smoothly for years to come, without costly repairs.

Trailer Boats -- Alex Zidock, Jr.

CHAPTER THIRTEEN
BATTERIES

Packed with electronics and powered by new-technology engines, boats of this generation demand more battery power than ever before. Many boats require two or more batteries. One cranking battery may be used to provide the short burst of energy required to fire-up the engine. Deep cycle batteries, are used for long-term operation of running lights, trolling motors, fish finders and laptop computers. Boaters are demanding better, more reliable marine batteries, and the industry is providing them, but, unless the boater practices good battery maintenance the boating experience could run out of power at the launch ramp.

The first thing every boater should understand about batteries is they are the same, but different. A battery designed for automotive use is different than a battery built for the marine environment. Will an automotive battery start an outboard engine? Yes, if it has enough cranking power. Will an automotive battery operate running lights, fish finders and the like? Again the answer is yes, but it will have a short life. Unlike automobile batteries, marine batteries are built to handle the bouncing ride of a boat trailer, and the pounding of the boat on the water. This is an important difference between the two, since one of the major causes for battery failure is vibration. Many marine batteries are also built with sealed cases, for virtually, leak-proof operation. There are other important differences too.

Figure 17
Courtesy of the manufacturer.

Deep cycle battery.

Marine, deep cycle batteries have thick internal plates covered with a high-density active material. The thick plates store energy that is released slowly during discharge while using a trolling motor or other electronic instruments. The high-density, active material stays in the plates grid structure longer, resisting normal cycling breakdown. Automotive batteries have thin plates covered with low-density active material. An automobile battery's primary job is to release a burst of energy long enough to turn the crankshaft, and to have sufficient power to charge the spark plugs, but only until the engine starts and the alternator takes over. The car battery's low-density, active material easily sheds from the plates when these batteries are exposed to the deep cycling punishment of boating applications.

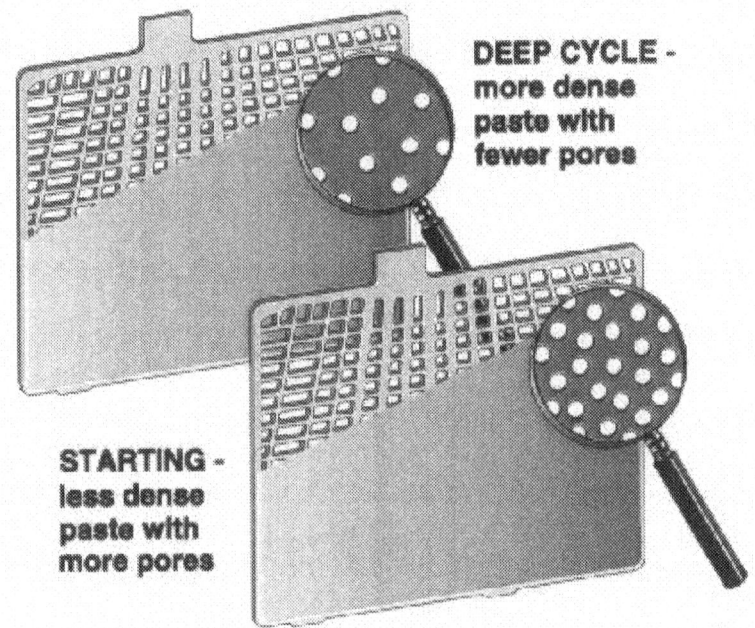

Figure 18
Courtesy of the manufacturer.

The differences in plate construction.

Companies have introduced batteries filled with a jelly-like acid instead of traditional liquid acid. Gel batteries last about twice as long as the conventional type but cost about three times as much. Gel batteries, however, have their own unique problems. Gel batteries are heavier, may affect boat performance, and need special care when recharging.

A marine batteries main components are as follows:

GRID: The most basic part of a battery is the grid. The grids are flat, rectangular, metal structures, used to hold the plate material and conduct current.

ELEMENTS: A plate group (element) is made by attaching a number of similar plates to a molten cast strap. Plate groups of opposite polarity are interlaced, so positive and negative plates alternate.

CASE: The case is made of lightweight material that is exceptionally strong and durable. One material commonly used is polypropylene. The battery case withstand shock and vibration.

ELECTROLYTE: In most batteries, the electrolyte consists of a solution of sulfuric acid (H_2SO_4) in water (H_2O). The solution is 36% acid and 64% water by weight. The electrolyte is measured by specific gravity. Specific gravity is the comparison of the weight of fluids with the weight of water. The electrolyte has a specific gravity of 1.270, commonly pronounced, "twelve seventy." This means, for equal volumes, the electrolyte weighs 1.270 times as much as water.

The Battery Council International (BCI) has set common designations on batteries to make it easier for consumers to identify battery sizes and power. Batteries in sizes 24 and 27 are, usually, the battery sizes in the marine battery group.

References to Cold Cranking Amps (CCA), is another BCI standardization which measures the discharge load a new, fully charged, lead-acid battery at 0^0 Fahrenheit (-17.8^0 Celsius) can continuously deliver for 30 seconds, while maintaining a voltage of 1.2 volts per cell. This is used to measure the battery power for starting automobile engines.

Marine batteries are measured by the BCI's Marine Cranking Amperes (MCA), which stands for the discharge load in amperes, the lead-acid battery at 32^0 Fahrenheit (0^0 Celsius) can deliver continuously for 30 seconds, while maintaining a terminal voltage of at least 1.2 volts per cell.

Ampere per hour (Ah) rating is important when

determining the type and number of batteries required to meet a boats specific need. Ah are measured in amps, at 80^0 Fahrenheit, and is the amount of current a battery can deliver, multiplied by the amount of hours, without falling below 1.75 volts per cell. Most marine, deep-cycle batteries are rated on a 20-hour discharge rate. If you have a 100 Ah battery, it will deliver 5 amps for 20 hours. (hours x amps = Ah). The RC rating of a battery has direct correlation with Ah. You can find the approximate Ah rating by multiplying the battery's RC rating by 0.6.

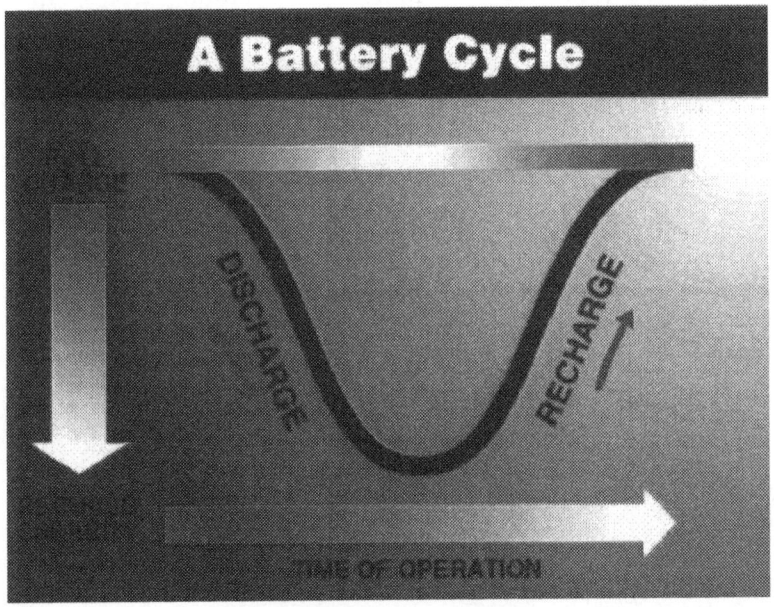

Figure 19
Courtesy of the manufacturer.

One cycle of a battery's life.

It is a simple task to replace the battery on your boat with the same type and power rating as the one that came with the boat. However, it's not always easy, since boaters seem to add accessory gadgets to make their boats more fishable and compatible with family activities.

To determine size and how many batteries you need on your boat, first determine your total power requirements and the approximate time those items will be used. Here's an example used in the Interstate Batteries' consumer brochure.

Typical accessories and the amount of amps each draws:

12 volt accessory	Amps	Hours	Ah
Lights	5	5	25
Depth Sounder (LCD)	5	1	5
Trolling Motor	10	5	50
Total Ah			80

For this setup, 80 Ah battery would provide the minimum requirements to handle these accessories. But, to assure acceptable battery cycle life and performance, divide 80 Ah by .50 (50% Depth of Discharge) to get 160 Ah. Using a battery system rated for 160 Ah @ 20 hour discharge rate will provide the correct power.

A cycle in a battery's life is one discharge and recharge of any depth. The amount of battery discharge (in percent) compared to fully charged is, appropriately, called battery depth of discharge (DOD). 50% DOD indicates a battery has been discharged by 50% of its total capacity and has a 50% charge left.

Trailer Boats -- Alex Zidock, Jr.

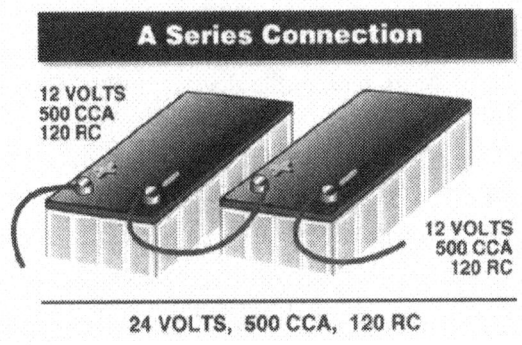

24 VOLTS, 500 CCA, 120 RC

Figure 20
Courtesy of the manufacturer.

Two 12 volt batteries connected to achieve 24 volts.

To match your battery power to your power need, or to increase voltage, batteries can be connected in different sequences. To achieve a parallel connection, attach a wire from the positive (+) to the positive (+) and the negative (-) to the negative (-). This configuration doubles the power, or amp hour, rating of the battery while maintaining the voltage. Connected this way, two 25-amp hour 12-volt batteries, in parallel, will produce a 50-amp hour, 12-volt system.

Sometimes, it is necessary to increase voltage, but keep the battery capacity the same. Batteries installed in a series accomplish just that. To end up with a 24-volt system you would connect one 12-volt battery's positive post to the second 12-volt battery's negative post.

If your boat requires only one battery, which will double as the power source to crank your engine, as well as supply power for running lights, bilge pump and other occasionally used power draws, your choice should be a deep cycle battery. Most marine, deep cycle batteries can handle the cranking duty, as well as the punishment of many deep discharges. It is not unusual for a deep cycle battery to be drained of its power completely, and be fully recharged hundreds of times. At best, an automotive battery is not built to handle deep cycling. It won't last more than a few deep discharges before it loses it's ability to take a charge, and fails completely.

How you charge your battery will determine the battery's life. Gel batteries are sensitive to high voltage charging (14.2 volts or more). While their design permits rapid charging even at low charge voltages, battery chargers and alternators with high charging voltages can damage gel batteries.

Here are some battery charging tips provided by one battery company that will work in most instances:

1. Choose the charger that matches the type of battery you intend to recharge, i.e., liquid electrolyte, marine/RV, automotive, maintenance-free and gel cell.

2. Match the proper battery voltage (6, 12, 24 or 36 volt)

3. Choose the charging amps. A good rule of thumb is a charger which will provide a maximum of 25 amps for each 100 Ah of the battery (20 amps per Ah on a sealed gel-deep cycle battery).

4. Select a charger with a capacity sufficient to fully recharge the batteries within eight to 12 hours.

5. It is recommended to use a charger which is timed or, automatically, shuts off when the battery reaches a full state of charge.

6. Always read and follow the charger instruction manual safety and procedural recommendations. Different manufacturers offer various features which may influence charging parameters.

Do not delay charging your batteries after use. Recharge as soon as possible after one day's use. Allowing the battery to sit discharged for several days may hamper its recharge acceptance, and ultimately, its performance.

Battery manufacturers are most helpful in providing information to consumers. Here are some frequently asked questions, taken from battery companies' consumer product brochures, and their web sites.

Q. *Which is the most detrimental to a battery, heat or cold?*

A. Both extremes create battery problems. Extreme heat will allow the battery to increase performance level for a short time. However, internally, it accelerates corrosion and other deterioration factors which lead to overall short battery life. Extreme cold temperatures within the battery result in a reduction of battery efficiency level, which reduces short term performance. (Interstate)

Q. *If I don't have any distilled water, is it OK to add tap water to my battery?*

A. Don't use tap or well water, as they may contain chlorine, iron or salts that will harm the battery. Use only distilled or de-ionized water. Most battery acid levels can be sufficiently restored with 16 ounces of distilled water, so keep at least that much on hand for each battery on your boat. (DieHard)

Q. *What is reserve capacity?*

A. Reserve capacity (RC) is the time required (in minutes) for a fully charged battery at 80^0 Fahrenheit (27.5^0 Celsius), under a constant 25 amp draw, to reach a voltage of 10.5 volts. In other words, this is the time the battery will continue to operate onboard accessories in the event of alternator failure. (Voyager)

Trailer Boats -- *Alex Zidock, Jr.*

Q. *I've seen anglers pour Coca-Cola on their battery terminals and posts to neutralize the corrosion buildup. Also I've heard people say if you drop an aspirin into each battery cell it will increase performance. Do these tricks work?*

A. Forget the aspirin right now. Don't put anything into your battery cells except distilled water. Don't do the coke thing either. Here's the recommended drill: Disconnect battery cable connectors. Clean ends of battery cables very thoroughly with a mixture of baking soda and water or ammonia and water. Use a steel wire brush to remove all the white crusty material. Make sure the inside of cable ends are clean. Clean battery posts thoroughly, reconnect cables to the battery. Coat the ends of the cables with a heavy coat of white grease. Do this every six months or whenever you get a buildup of crusty white stuff. (DieHard)

Q. *Do marine/RV-deep cycle batteries develop a memory?*

A. No! Lead-acid batteries do not develop a memory like rechargeable camera batteries. What does this mean to you? Lead-acid batteries have the ability to cycle to various amounts of depth of discharge (DOD) anytime during their service life without a memory developing inside the battery. (Interstate)

Q. *What are the best methods for checking a battery's charge?*

A. The best way to check a battery's charge is to use a hydrometer. A fully charged battery will have a specific gravity level of 1.265 to 1.280 per cell. Remove the vent caps and check each cell for specific gravity levels. If the specific gravity is less than this level, it should be recharged prior to use. If you have added water, the battery needs to be recharged prior to testing with a hydrometer.

    A second method of testing the battery's state of charge is to use a digital voltmeter. A good quality, fully charged battery will have a voltage reading of 12.72 after resting for twenty-four hours. If you have a gel battery, its vents cannot be opened; therefore, you can't check the specific gravity and must use a digital voltmeter. (DieHard)

Trailer Boats -- *Alex Zidock, Jr.*

CHAPTER FOURTEEN
PROPELLERS

My neighbor returned from a huge flea market with a couple of used propellers - one three-bladed, and the other four. He said they "looked about the size" of the one on his 19-foot stern dive. "After what I paid to replace the prop I busted last spring, these were a steal," he said. Justifying his purchase he continued, "The guy who sold them to me said as long as they fit on the shaft they'll be O.K. Besides, if they didn't fit, I could bring them back."

He and I immediately had a conversation about propeller size, pitch and their effect on his engine's speed. After a glancing match-up with his stock prop, we could see these look-a-likes were smaller in diameter, pitched wrong and, obviously, not for his boat. In a short time the two "real deal wheels" were rumbling around in the bed of his pickup, headed back to the flea market.

Finding a good, used propeller for your motor isn't easy. To be safe you should exactly match the one that was stock with your rig when it was new. In most cases, the manufacturer of your engine/boat, whether it is an outboard, inboard or stern drive, has determined which propeller will give you adequate, all-around performance, while keeping your engine within its safe rpm parameters. That's the easy way, particularly if you use your boat for many purposes. However, if you use your boat for one specific activity, such as water skiing or fishing, you can improve the performance of your boat and motor by changing or altering your current propeller. This requires knowledge, trial and error. Even though propeller manufacturing has gone high tech, it's still not rocket science, and educated, experimentation is the key.

Pleasure boating propellers are hand-crafted of softer materials and then passed on to a tool and die maker who creates a mold. Hot metals are poured in the molds to mass produce the props. Some new props are designed on the computer with a CAD (Computer Aided Design) program. Once designed the computer can create the die through an NC (numerically controlled) machine. This machine converts digital data into a metal part, or mold.

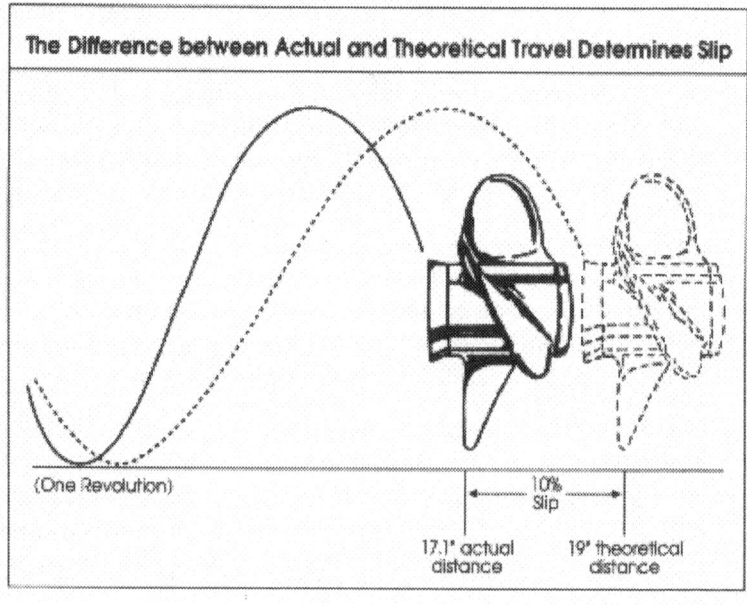

Figure 21
Courtesy of the manufacturer.

Trailer Boats -- *Alex Zidock, Jr.*

Even with modern technology in manufacturing, there are many other factors that relate to the performance of a propeller. The hull design of the boat has a tremendous effect on the efficiency a propeller can achieve. That's why it's important to match a motor and propeller to a specific boat. Small differences from one blade to the next, can cause a variation in performance or unacceptable cavitation. The result of cavitation can be seen in a photo taken of a fast moving boat propeller, which shows a stream of bubbles in a spiral-like trail.

According to *Chapman Piloting, Seamanship and Small Boat Handling*, "cavitation occurs when a high-speed propeller loses its bite in the water, creating a partial vacuum, loss of thrust, and excessive shaft speed; continued cavitation can result in excessive blade wear." As the propeller blade cuts through the water at high speed, vapor forms on the low-pressure side of the blade. The water pressure drops so low the water molecules actually explode, or boil, as they break apart violently and leave a trail of bubbles. The vaporization causes the propeller to speed up, losing contact with the water, which slows the boat. This effect causes the vapor to recondense into a liquid that erodes the surfaces of the blades and lower unit. It causes the pitting you may have seen in the black paint on your prop blades. Every prop experiences some cavitation on the back or non-working side, and near the blade tips. More cup in a blade tip can reduce the effects of cavitation. Adding cup, simply means, the tip of the propeller blades are curled to form a more rounded or cupped edge. This must be done at a propeller shop. Cupping a propeller adds bite in the water and aids the prop in getting better traction when the motor is tilted slightly up while running in shallow water.

Most boaters are familiar with the horizontal, flat piece of metal located near the bottom of the lower unit, just above the propeller. This is called the anti-cavitation or anti-ventilation plate. Its purpose is to direct the water coming off the blades, downward.

A propeller is basically a screw, and in slang, is even referred to as such. Some also call them wheels. To understand the terminology and technology of a propeller, think of it as a screw going through a piece of wood. Picture it as a modified, cross-section of one of the threads of the screw. The angle of the threads, or of the blades in this case, is called pitch. The pitch of the propeller is measured by how far the propeller would travel in one revolution if there were no slip. As a traditional screw goes through wood, there is no slip because the wood is hard. But as a propeller goes through the water, the bite is not as solid, so there is a certain amount of slip. However, if there were no slip, a 19-inch pitch propeller would move the boat exactly 19-inches forward for every revolution it made. A propeller with a 15-inch diameter and 19-inch pitch would be identified as a 15 inch x 19 pitch, or simply, a 15 x 19 prop.

Determining what diameter, pitch and blade configuration propeller is best suited for your boat relies on how you use your boat. If you use your boat in an average way, fishing in the morning, water skiing in the afternoon and as a party barge later in the day, the best propeller is probably the one that came with the rig. It may not give you optimum results in all of those applications, but it will give you average performance for each activity.

The ideal propeller for any boat/motor used for a specific application is the one that allows the motor to achieve its full rated rpm when the boat is trimmed out and operated at Wide Open Throttle (WOT). A propeller that turns too quickly is too small. It will not develop its full power potential and will exceed the engine manufacturer's top rpm rating, and may damage the engine. The safest is to fall within 250 rpm of the factory-suggested, maximum rpm rating. Better yet, hit the numbers right on.

To check if a propeller is right for your boat/motor combination, operate your boat with a light load. Use about a half tank of fuel with one person on board. Slowly, bring the boat to full throttle while checking the tachometer. In the operating manual that came with your motor, the manufacturer will tell you that the motor should operate between certain rpm for best performance. With a light load, the rpm on the tachometer should be near the maximum recommended number. If the rpm is too high, switch to a propeller with a higher pitch. If the engine speed is too low, replace the prop with one of a lower pitch. Changing the pitch of a propeller by 2-inches will result in a change of about 300 to 400 rpm. Fishermen and the cruising boater, looking for higher top speeds and better fuel economy, would seek a higher pitched prop. On the other hand, water skiers looking for a fast hole shot, a lower pitched prop would fill the need.

It is customary for manufacturers to supply three-bladed, aluminum props with motors. Props made of other materials such as bronze, stainless steel and nonmetal composite materials are available and manufactured for specific applications. They are made in different diameters, with two, three, four or more blades.

Propeller hubs are different too. On smaller motors the prop hub is equipped with a shear pin made of soft metal. The shear pin locks the propeller shaft to the propeller. A nut with a hole through it is screwed onto the propeller shaft until the hole in the nut and the hole in the propeller shaft are aligned. A cotter pin is inserted to keep the nut from backing off. If the propeller hits a rock or other solid object, the soft pin is sheared off on both ends before the sudden impact can be transmitted to the internal gears of the motor. The other type of hub found on motors is one with a built-in slip clutch. It consists of a rubber bushing or hub inside the outer hub, which, when under normal use, transfers the power from the shaft to the propeller, but slips with sudden impact on one of the blades. Most small, outboard motors have a place inside the motor cowl to store extra cotter pins and shear pins.

    Stainless steel wheels are, probably, the ultimate in performance and are usually found on high speed or racing boats. Of course, they are the most expensive. A three-bladed stainless prop will cost about twice the price of an aluminum prop. Stainless steel is strong, durable and can be made much thinner, reducing drag and boosting performance over aluminum or composite props. The stainless propeller will withstand more punishment without damage, and, because it can be reshaped without breaking, as the softer aluminum prop might, it is easier to repair.

    Not quite as expensive as stainless steel, but more expensive and stronger than aluminum, bronze propellers also have the ability to be easily reshaped after damage. Bronze screws are mostly found on larger saltwater boats.

There are more than two dozen manufacturers of traditional boat propellers. Newer to the marketplace is a modular design, nonmetallic propeller made of a composite of fiberglass, nylon and resin, in which blades can easily be removed and changed. Not only are these propellers fairly inexpensive, their unique design allows boaters to change individual blades on a prop, should one get damaged, reducing the cost of repairs. Blades can also be replaced to change pitch. With that in mind, a boater can carry more than one set of blades, using one set for fishing and a second set, with a different pitch, for water skiing or for emergency use. These propellers are made to fit a wide variety of boats/motors, from 9.9 to 260 h.p. Owners of small boats, who often operate in shallow water, or beach-launch their boats, find it easy to repair a broken prop on the spot. One particular manufacturer of composite propellers even places a lifetime, unconditional replacement guarantee on the propeller hubs.

Figure 22
Courtesy of the manufacturer.

Typical prop with replaceable blades.

Trailer Boats -- *Alex Zidock, Jr.*

When you consider the propeller is the only connection between the power on your boat and the water, it should command attention. Trying new designs, altering or repairing your current propeller can increase performance and speed, plus increase your gas mileage. The wrong propeller or one even slightly damaged can cause you to lose at least one gallon of gas for every four you burn. Continuing to operate a boat with a badly damaged blade can wreak havoc with your engine's lower unit.

Propellers can cost about $160 for a standard three-bladed aluminum model and $600 or more for a precision, stainless steel prop. If you come across a good, used propeller at a local flea market, do what I do. On the back of that little piece of paper you carry in your wallet, the one that has your significant other's clothes and ring sizes, jot down the sizes of the propellers your boat will accept. Now you won't end up with a large paperweight, sporting Mickey Mouse ears.

CHAPTER FIFTEEN
BILGE PUMPS

Dock space was at a premium in the late 1960s, and I was a young man with little extra money. That being the case, I opted to put my first big boat on a mooring buoy in the Delaware River, just south of Pennsbury Manor, the restored Bucks County home of William Penn. She was a mature, 21-foot day cruiser, built of wood, but she was all mine. I spent countless hours in a labor of love, scraping, caulking, painting and fixing her up before our first launch. It was because I wanted to get an early start on the 4th of July weekend, and the fact, I worry a lot, that my pride and joy didn't end up as sunken debris less than a month after the launch.

As I reached the dock that morning and headed for a yacht club dinghy, I glanced across the river to see my boat pulling hard on the 15-foot nylon pennant that ran from the bow eye to the buoy. At first I thought there might be an exceptionally strong current. Then I noticed the boat was riding lower in the water than usual. I soon realized my boat was sinking, and I had better get to her fast.

I learned two lessons that day. One was, old wooden boats (even newer ones with encapsulated wood stringers) get dry-rot which causes leaks. And the other lesson, the cheapest insurance for any boat owner, is the cost it takes to purchase and install the largest bilge pump that will, realistically, fit on a boat. My old wooden boat stayed afloat only because I worried the original pump might quit someday. During my initial spring fitting-out, I installed a back up pump. The mistake I made was installing a slightly smaller bilge pump than the original. I was lucky, even though some heavy rain added extra bilge water when a corner snap on the canvas popped loose, the smaller pump still saved the day when the larger one quit.

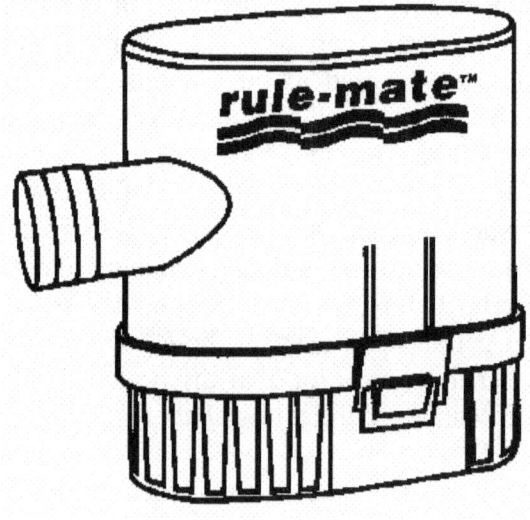

Figure 23
Courtesy of the manufacturer.

Typical electric bilge pump.

Bilge pumps come in a variety of sizes for a variety of applications. If you are one of those who think your boat is too small for any type of bilge pump, you obviously place little value on your boat. In some very small boats, hand bailers or manual bilge pumps may suit the need. The accepted rule (this may not apply to larger boats) is, the boat optimally be equipped with a bilge pump that can handle 100 gallons per hour (gph) per foot of boat. A 20-foot boat should have a bilge pump rated to pump 2000 gph, or two bilge pumps rated at 1000 gph each.

Figure 24
Courtesy of the manufacturer.

This typical hand operated pump can be used as an emergency backup when the need arises.

When you want to add a bilge pump to a small boat, or if you are replacing a bilge pump on a small boat, it isn't the best deal to buy a small pump. Remember, it only takes a little water to sink a little boat.

To understand why bilge pumps are so important you first must realize no matter the size or type of boat you have, (except pontoon boats) the place all excess water, grease, oil, and other debris gathers is in the bottom of the boat. That's called the bilge. If you have a floor, or sole, in your boat, the bilge is below the floor. For those who always trailer their boat, the bilge is usually emptied when the drain plug is removed, but a bilge pump is still necessary in case the hull springs a leak, or the boat takes water over the gunwale while afloat.

Even though boats have an electrically operated bilge pump it's a good idea to have a manually operated bilge pump on board. More then 40 years ago Beckson Marine developed a manual bilge pump that first was made with a gold anodized, aluminum body. In 1957, when the technology for making PVC had been refined, Beckson modified their original design and produced the first, self-priming, all-plastic pump, and, possibly the first all-plastic machine, in the world.

Improvements on the Beckson design have led to a pump that can be manually operated to move 30 gallons of water per minute, which is approximately 1800 gph. The pump can be mounted in a permanent position, or left free to be used where it's most needed. In an emergency, a hand-operated pump can save your boat from going to the bottom.

Most manufacturers of boats install bilge pumps at the factory when they build the boat. The type pump normally installed is a simple device with a sealed electric motor, an enclosed impeller, and a discharge nozzle. The base of the pump draws water into the impeller. On larger, more powerful bilge pumps, there may be an intake hose. On the side of the unit there is usually a float which operates a switch that automatically turns the pump off and on. Some bilge pumps are wired directly to a panel switch on the boat's dash, and the boat operator manually turns the switch on and off.

Now there are even computerized bilge pumps. These pumps start themselves when there is water around the impeller. The impeller recognizes the presence of water by amp draw. Electronics measure the amp load, and if the amp load is high enough, keeps the pump running. When the water is gone the pump feels no resistance and the impeller shuts off.

One positive side of this new technology is the pump requires a smaller foot print than the old float switch pump, which means the new style pumps can be positioned in more confined areas.

The other advantage of the computer pump over the pump with a float, is the float can be hung up with debris, causing it to malfunction. With any style bilge pump, there must be good housekeeping rules in the bilge area. Grease, oil and other petroleum products accumulate on switches and in the pump. These products are not very compatible with bilge pumps and their wires. All connections should be solderless, crimp connectors with heat shrink tubing over the connection .

While it's a great idea to install a boat battery as low in the bilge as possible for stability, it's a bad idea for safety. If a boat begins to take on water and the battery gets too wet, it will short out and stop the pump.

Another common problem with bilge pumps occurs with the hoses. As the outlet hose rises the efficiency of the pump decreases. As an example, a 360 gph pump will pump 360 gph at the pump opening, but if the hose from the pump rises 3.5 feet to reach the through-hull fitting, the pump will only push 265 gph through the hose. If you take the hose up 7 feet, the rate drops to 190 gph. Rise is important because these are not self-priming pumps. The position of the discharge hose is all-important to keeping the prime. All discharge hoses continually run upward. Gravity pulling the water back down into the pump for backpressure will keep the pump primed. Replacement of hoses or new installations should be made so there are no loops, bellies, or long horizontal runs which could leave room for air to be trapped. It's also a good idea to keep the discharge hose steep and as short as possible.

Since the bilge is the collector of most unwanted things that enter a boat, there could be danger to the environment as well as to the operator and passengers. Refueling may cause gasoline to be spilled into the boat. Changing, adding or mixing oil can cause spills, which will find their way to the bilge. When water is mixed with these liquids, the bilge pump can dump these unwanted pollutants into the environment. If you suspect petroleum has found its way into your bilge, take extreme care the fumes from these flammables don't cause an explosion. Larger boats are equipped with bilge blowers that should be engaged before the engine is started. Never turn on a bilge pump to deliver these unwanted liquids overboard.

As a normal part of boat maintenance, the bilge should be cleaned every season or when there is an accidental spill of gas or oil in the boat. Remove any large debris by hand. An easy method to clean gas and oil that sticks in the bilge is to put about a pint of liquid, laundry detergent and a quart of household, chlorine bleach in a five gallon bucket. Add at least four gallons of water and dump all of it into your bilge, depending on the size of your boat. Disconnect, or turn off your bilge pump. Be careful not to get the bleach on any boat fabric or carpeting. If your boat is on a trailer, let the solution slosh around in the bilge while you drive the boat to or from the launch ramp. Follow the same procedure if your boat is in a slip, but instead of letting the solution slosh around during the drive, a few hours of wave motion will slosh the liquid around the bilge. Disconnect the bilge discharge hose from the through hull fitting, put it in an empty five-gallon bucket and turn on the bilge pump. Collect the bilge water in the bucket and dispose of it properly. Do not allow this mixture to be dumped overboard. Then rinse the bilge with fresh water. There are other products such as special oil socks and cleaners that also work well to clean the bilge.

If you think your bilge pump is not working properly, especially after you've fixed, repaired or replaced it, check the wiring. If you wire a bilge pump backwards, (positive on negative and negative on positive) the pump will still work, but only at 20 per cent efficiency. If you reduce the size of the discharge hose from the size of the pump outlet you decrease the output of water by as much. Conversely, if you increase the size of the discharge hose from the size of the pump outlet, you gain nothing.

Unfortunately, most owners of small boats rarely look into their boat's bilge until there's trouble. Holes that appear in the lower edges of the floors and the frames next to the keel allow bilge water to flow freely from the bow to the stern, and then allow the fluids to flow to the lowest part of the bilge, are called limber holes.

Trailer Boats -- Alex Zidock, Jr.

Trailer Boats -- *Alex Zidock, Jr.*

CHAPTER SIXTEEN
SONAR & FISH FINDERS

There's nothing wrong with sitting on the bank of a river or lake with a fishing rod, a worm on the hook, and nothing more to do but watch the bobber drift with the current. For weekend fishermen and serious anglers, there is a wide variety of magic boxes on the market that can provide an extra measure of boating safety, as well as help put more fish in the livewell. Call them depth finders, flashers, or fishfinders, they're all related, sonar devices that range from the very simple, to the most elaborate, computer-driven technology the space-age can offer. Somewhere between the bobber and the satellite there's a unit for your boat.

Sonar (an acronym for SOund, NAvigation and Ranging) was developed in the early 1940s, during World War II, to detect submarines. The device sends a pulse of ultrasonic energy from a boat to the bottom of the water, and then registers the sound as it bounces back up to the boat. If the beam hits something on the way to the bottom, it sends the sound back quicker. Since we know sound travels through water at approximately 4,800 feet per second, (1,100 feet per second through air) it's a matter of calculation to determine how far the bottom is by how long it takes the sound to make a round trip. The information is then transformed, electronically onto different types of displays for easy reading.

Early depth sounders took the sound signal, transformed it into an electrical pulse that fired a neon light that moved around a clock-like scale, marked off in fathoms or feet. This type of unit is called a flasher. The more solid the bottom structures, the stronger the signal. If a smaller, less dense object, like a fish got in the way of the sound beam, a weaker signal was returned. Using the combination of information, the business of developing fish-finding sonar for recreational fishermen, was born.

Fish finders have come a long way since 1957, when Darrell Lowrance, and his father Carl, founded Lowrance Electronics, Inc., and introduced transistorized, portable sonars to anglers around the world. According to Lowrance, Darrell and his brother Arlen were among the first inland divers to use SCUBA gear. Their underwater explorations taught them fish were not randomly scattered in lakes and rivers, but were generally found in schools and confined to specific areas, where food, cover, preferred water temperatures, or oxygen levels prevailed. They set out to develop a sonar fishfinder that was portable and contained its own batteries. Their first successful unit was a flasher, packaged in a little green box they called *Fish LO-K-TORs*.

Other companies also began making fishfinders, but the early technology was comparatively expensive and only the most serious, well-heeled anglers used fishfinders. Today, for about the cost of a good rod, reel and a package of flavored plastic baits, an angler can purchase a fish finder. As one popular manufacturer states, "Delivers big dollar performance at a small dollar price."

Even if a boat is purchased for water skiing or cruising and no fishing will take place from the boat, a depth finder is a must. Every captain must know how deep the water is to prevent the boat from running aground. The depth finder is not only important to use when the boat is underway in deeper water, but also extremely important to use when the boat will be beached or anchored in shallow water. Rainfall and tides determine the depths of many rivers, lakes and bays. The rise and lowering of the water level may bring submerged objects closer to the water surface than normal. Without some way of reading the contour of the bottom, a boater can easily get into trouble.

Today's modern fish finders/depth sounders give anglers and boaters a clear picture of what's in the water and on the bottom. Most finders read only from the bottom of the boat straight down to the bottom of the water, and signal anything in between. Some fish finders will also read what's on either side of the boat. They're called 'side-finders.' Other, much more expensive units, have the ability to read what is ahead of the boat. Several manufacturers incorporate many features into one unit. Most finders provide information as water temperature, vessel speed, direction, digital depth read-outs, are compatibility with Global Positioning Systems (GPS), and have the ability to interact with onboard PCs for interaction with special navigational and sophisticated nautical chart programs.

Industry statistics show only about half the fishermen in this country own a fish finder, but nearly every boat now manufactured has a depth finder installed when it leaves the factory. Of those that own the fish-finding units, only 50 percent use them regularly. Some of the reasons fishermen give for not owning the units is they are too expensive, and are too complicated to use. Once boaters get accustomed to using the depth finders, they become as conscious of them as the fuel gauge.

All fishfinder units are depth finders. But there are units available just for finding the depth, but are not as useful for finding fish. Both units are not very expensive. Actually, there are good units on the market for under $100. Most fish finders are preprogrammed to allow the user time for practical experience on the water to understand how the unit works.

A lack of knowledge can lead to improper installation of a fishfinder/depth finder, which in turn can cause the unit to malfunction. The basic components in any depth or fishfinder includes the transducer, which sends and receives the signal, an amplifier to enhance the signal, a device to perform the timing function and a visual, display monitor to display the information. Picture a flashlight mounted to the underside of a boat pointed directly toward the bottom. Compare the flashlight to the transducer, and the beam of light to the transducer's projected cone of sound. The closer the light beam is to the flashlight, the narrower the beam. The further the light beam must travel toward the bottom of the water, the wider it gets. Placement of the transducer is all-important.

The transducer is a small, usually streamlined, piece of hard ceramic, measuring a few inches across and about an inch thick. For most applications, the transducer should be mounted on the outside of the hull, at the bottom of the transom, near but not directly at the center of the boat. Through-hull mounting is also effective, but the most important thing to remember is to mount the transducer where air bubbles or cavitation will not occur. Air is not a good conductor of sound. The bubbles can act as an insulation and cut performance of your fishfinder dramatically. If the transducer is not mounted in a vertical position to the bottom of the water, the echo will bounce away and not be easily recorded.

Consideration should also be given to where the monitor will be mounted. Many bass boats have two finder monitors and two transducers. One monitor is usually mounted near the helm station, which may be used for general navigation, and the other at the front of the boat where it can be easily seen when the fisherman is operating a bow-mounted, electric trolling motor. Direct sunlight can interfere with some manufacturer's monochromatic, liquid crystal display (LCD) screens.

The screens of LCD fishfinders/depth finders are made of units called pixels. Each square pixel becomes dark or black when an electronic signal is sent to the monitor. A group of pixels may take the shape of a fish or school of baitfish. A row of attached pixels usually represents the bottom. The more expensive the fishfinder, the larger the screen and the more pixels, which in turn means more definition of objects that pass under the boat.

Some of the more expensive finders have a cathode ray tube (CRT) as their display monitor. The CRT produces a sharp image in monotones or full color much like a television set. The CRT finders are popular among owners of larger boats and captains of fishing charter fleets. The color screen makes it easier to distinguish between individual fish, schools of baitfish and the bottom. Fishfinders are not infallible but they're pretty darn accurate.

An average fishfinder sends out about four pings a second, and does not record unless it receives at least two pings back. It can miss fish, if a fish swims very quickly through the sonar signal near the surface, where the cone-shaped signal is narrow. Today's modern units can read the bottom and indicate if the bottom is hard or soft.

The best advice is to purchase a unit with only the features you want and to read the instructions thoroughly. A fish/depth finder can be a very important safety addition and it will add to your fishing success.

Figure 25
Courtesy of the manufacturer.

Typical LCD display.

Trailer Boats -- Alex Zidock, Jr.

CHAPTER SEVENTEEN
FITTING OUT & COSMETIC CARE

Ah, Spring! Or maybe you've put your boat in storage for several months and are now ready to put it back in service. Whatever the case, when you pull the cover off the boat you may be in for some surprises. Lifting the canvas may reveal remnants from winter hibernation or just an undisturbed rest. You may be surprised to find your boat has become a home for a variety of little critters that have left their marks on canvas, fiberglass and aluminum. Leaves that went unnoticed when you put your boat away, have created tough, tannic patterns on canvas and gelcoat and that's only the beginning.

The task of getting your boat ready for launch is at hand. The owners of bigger boats and yachts call this rite of spring, fitting out. It may not be a spring commissioning but just the same, when you take your boat out of storage there's usually work to be done. Whatever you call it, no matter the size of your boat, if it's aluminum, fiberglass, car-topper or trailerable, this initial fitting out is very important in many ways. This annual once-over will keep your boat looking good, maintain its value and keep it running trouble-free during peak fun times.

Even if you don't live in the north where this 'rite of spring' is tradition, you still may put your boat into long-term storage but your 'rite of spring' could be anytime of the year. Unless you use your boat all year long, and do regular maintenance, you should take time for a 'rite of spring' at least once a year.

If you kept your boat outdoors last winter you should have rigged a cover with a large tarp. This should have been supported in such a fashion it would hold the heavy winter snow and ice, and let water run off. A tent-type tarp allows the boat and canvas cover to breath, keeping condensation to a minimum. The tarp also protects the canvas cover from the elements, bird droppings, small branches and twigs. Commercially applied boat wrap works well, and if you can...do it, but it can be costly and it can't be reused.

Figure 26
Courtesy of the manufacturer.

The plastic cover will help protect the boat's canvas mooring cover.

After you remove the tarp, wash it, dry it, and fold it neatly for next year's use. Before you remove the boat's canvas cover, check it for wear at all stress points. Bird droppings on canvas can easily be cleaned with canvas cleaner or mild soap, sponge and hose. Before attacking those soiled spots, it's best to try a little cleaner or soap on an inconspicuous area to make sure it will not discolor the canvas. Once you've cleaned and dried the canvas, you may want to spray on a coat of waterproofing. Follow the directions on the container. Allow the treatment to dry before the canvas is put to use or folded for storage.

The next step is to thoroughly wash the boat. You may have cleaned the scum from the bottom when you put the boat up for the winter, but wash it again. Remove any loose or easy-to-undo items such as cushions, portable seats, cup holders and rod holders from the boat. This will make cleaning a lot easier. You should have removed the drain plug in the fall to allow any water to drain out of the hull during storage. Make sure leaves and other debris have not plugged the hole. Check the bilge pump. Is working freely? Check through-hull fittings for blockage.

Boat surfaces are unlike surfaces found in homes. While some combinations of household detergents may work, stick with the products made for boat surfaces. In most cases, boat surfaces are not like automobile surfaces either. Cleaners and polishing agents used in homes or on automobiles can damage gelcoat and other materials found on boats. Household cleaners, especially dish washing detergents, are highly alkaline and will streak fiberglass and marine paint. Boat wash, made specifically for marine surfaces, has a neutral pH and will safely wash away surface accumulations without leaving a residue. Do it right the first time or pay later.

Unpainted or untreated aluminum boats, or unpainted surfaces on pontoon boats will form a dusty residue no matter what you use to wash or clean the boat. This oxidation of untreated aluminum is a normal process.

If, after you've washed the boat, and the gelcoat or paint still has a powder-like haze, deterioration and oxidation has begun. You can use a variety of rubbing compounds made for gelcoat or painted surfaces to remove the oxidation, but go easy. Course compounds can quickly cut through the boats finish. A better option is a good quality fiberglass color restorer with sealer and a liquid polish, or paste wax. But, once again, not the same one you use on the family sedan, but one purchased specifically for marine use. Car polish will leave a film on the surface of the boat, and it will not protect the boat surface as well as one made for the marine environment.

There are few products that have been established as automotive, household cleaners or restorers that can be used effectively for boat maintenance. Road tar can be removed by dabbing the deposits with a cloth wetted with linseed oil. Let the spots stand until they soften. Dampen with the oil again, if needed, then take the same wet cloth and wipe off the tar. Wash the linseed oil off before proceeding.

If your boat has a windshield, keeping the wiper blades in good condition will prevent scratches on the windshield.

While there are a variety of good marine products available for cleaning and restoring vinyl, products like Armor-All are all-around gems for keeping rubber or vinyl looking like new once it has been cleaned with a product made for that purpose. Armor-All works on nearly everything rubber, vinyl, plastic, Plexiglas and even sealed wood and finished leather. It will keep trailer tires from cracking and protect trailer rollers from the elements. Don't use a vinyl protector on surfaces where you stand, step, need good footing, or on wooden bench seats in small boats. It's not good to use on controls, such as steering wheels, or other areas where slippery surfaces could be dangerous for safe operation of the boat. There are marine products specifically made for these applications. While Armor-All may work in some instances, don't use harsh household cleaners on vinyl's. Cleaners made specifically for marine vinyl are formulated not to remove plasticizers (those added agents which keep vinyl soft and pliable) and, therefore, will not contribute to vinyl degradation. Most general household cleaners will cause vinyl to harden and eventually crack.

Boat running lights and the lights on your trailer, which occasionally get submerged, are particularly vulnerable to corrosion. With switches off, remove the lenses carefully, then the bulb. If the bulb is difficult coming out, spray it with WD-40 and let it set a while. If you still have a problem, or if the bulb loosens from the base, you may need a pair of pliers to get the base out of the socket. If the bulb is intact, polish the contacts with bronze wool. Before reassembly, spray the socket with CRC or another corrosion blocker. While you are inspecting and cleaning the bulbs, check the wires. If old electrical tape is coming loose, try liquid electrical tape or crimp connectors and heat shrink tubing.

While you're checking the lights on your boat trailer, you might as well check the tow ball on the tow vehicle and socket on the trailer. If the ball is rusty, shine it up with steel wool and apply a light film of grease on the ball. Dab a finger-full of grease in the socket. Use the same grease you pack in the trailer's wheel bearings. Does the winch work freely? And what about the cable or strap? Clean and spray CRC in the electrical harness that provides power to your trailer from the tow vehicle.

When you're ready to begin refitting your, boat check each item carefully before you put it back on board. Check all dock lines and replace any that look frayed. Determine if your anchor, anchor line and rode are in good condition. For line ends that are frayed, dip the frayed end of the line into whipping liquid. When the product dries it makes a neat end and prevents further unraveling. The liquid rope whip comes in colors so you can easily distinguish between different lines.

Fire extinguishers and flares may need to be recharged or replaced if they are out of date. Check, repair or replace any items you carry in your first aid container. Does your whistle or horn work? How about the flashlight bulb and batteries, spare fuses, sheer pins, emergency paddle and tools?

In most states, you must have PFDs for everyone on your boat. Check each life preserver and make sure all of the belts and buckles are secure and in good working order. Don't skimp here. Safety is one of the most important elements when boating. Replace any PFDs, life jackets or life preservers that are questionable. If the jackets are moldy, use a marine mold and mildew cleaner to restore them.

Hopefully, you put your outboard away last fall after completing routine fogging and storage maintenance, so firing it up this spring shouldn't be a chore. Make sure spark plugs are in tight, the mice have not built a nest in the carburetor or blower hoses, and all controls and steering cables work freely. Wipe out spider webs and egg sacks from under the outboard's cover. If you did not replace oil in the lower unit of the engine in the fall you should do it now. If your engine has electric start, or if you run an electric motor, you'll want to make sure your battery is in tiptop shape. Use a hydrometer to check the cells, if your battery is not maintenance-free type. You may need to add distilled water. Use a wire brush to clean battery terminals and cable ends. A light application of grease on the posts will retard corrosion.

You may not have thoroughly inspected the propeller before, so now is a good time to look for dings and bent blades. Badly bent propellers should be repaired or replaced. Even small nicks and minor bends can affect long range propeller and boat performance. Most of the time you can file nicks out of the blades, or lightly tap the bend back in shape with a hammer, and it will work just fine. You should remove the propeller to work on it. Check the propeller hub and splines for wear. Protect your engine by applying a coat of good marine wax.

Small boat? Big boat? Your list for fitting out may be longer or shorter, but the last line should read, "put in the drain plug."

Boaters who trailer their boats enjoy a multitude of lakes and rivers, on which they fish from their boats, water ski or just plain enjoy boating and cruising. Traveling from place to place, our boats encounter a variety of conditions that may affect the boat cosmetically, or may, more seriously, hamper the boats reliability or performance. For many of us, messing around with our boats on those first warm days of spring is important fun. Year-round maintenance is a smart practice, but what you do this spring, or after any long-term storage but before the initial launch, will go a long way to keep your boat looking good and provide you a safe, carefree time on the water all boating season.

Trailer Boats -- *Alex Zidock, Jr.*

Trailer Boats -- Alex Zidock, Jr.

CHAPTER EIGHTEEN
PRE-SEASON MOTOR MAINTENANCE

Starting your boat motor for the first time in the spring or after an extended storage period, should be easy if you did a little preventative maintenance before you put it to bed. No matter if your outboard motor was stored indoors or outdoors, if it is under 10-hp or over 200-hp, a preseason checkup will help keep it running trouble-free. It's the kind of work you can do yourself with just a few tools.

A Spring checkup for any boat motor is a must, but nothing beats regular preventive maintenance. In northern states, where boats are taken out of service during the winter months, you must do good maintenance in the fall before you store your boat and motor to prevent major problems in the Spring.

You don't have to be a fisherman to get fishing line wrapped around your propeller. If fishing line tangled around the propeller shaft last season and was allowed built up behind the stopper, it could cut into the water seal and allow water to get into the lower unit. The water that has found its way into the lower unit's house could freeze, expand and break expensive parts in the lower unit.

However anxious you may be to get on the water, save time later by spending a little time commissioning giving your boat motor a good, once-over. If you have an outboard motor, you should visually inspect it with the cowling cover on, and then with it off. It doesn't hurt to wash your motor to get rid of any dirt, spider webs or other debris that may have accumulated during storage. Be careful not to get water inside the engine, being extra careful around the carburetor air intakes. It's a good idea to touchup the nicks and scratches on metal parts, since they are areas where corrosion will begin.

Grease areas around shift levers, steering brackets and the propeller shaft, or wherever you find a grease fitting. Use a good marine-grade, water-resistant grease.

If your outboard engine is started manually with a rope, slowly pull the cord out of the recoil starter assembly and check it for wear or fraying. If it shows wear, it should be replaced with a new cord designed for that function. Most electric start outboard motors provide for emergency manual starting by winding a length of rope around a notched pulley on top of the engine. Make sure your tool kit has a length of rope, the correct diameter, which can be used during emergency starting situations.

Spark plugs are inexpensive, but can cause a lot of problems. A spare set should also be in your tool kit. It's best to get into the habit of replacing the plugs once a year. If you're frugal and figure a little cleanup will do, don't use a spark plug cleaning device that blasts the plugs with sand. The sharp edges on the sand are meant to cut off burned-on gas and oil. Unless you get every grain of sand out of the cavity of the spark plug, and from around the electrode, sand can get into your engine and scratch or score cylinder walls, causing damage, excessive wear, and eventually loss of compression.

Old plugs or new, if they are a conventional J-plug, the gap needs to be set with a gauge. Spark plug gauges are inexpensive and can be found at any automotive store. Look in your manual for correct spark plug gap settings.

Some outboard engines use surface-gap spark plugs. These plugs will fire in a much richer gas/oil mixture, where the traditional J-plug will foul. Gasoline, like its cousin, oil, is also a lubricant. Certain engines are purposely built to overload the cylinder with the gas/oil mixture to insure proper lubrication of internal motor parts. If your motor came with the surface-gap type spark plug, that's the best choice for your motor. It is not a good idea to use spark plugs not recommended by the manufacturer.

If you removed all the gasoline from inside your outboard motor in the fall, you should not have a problem with carburetor or fuel lines in the spring. If your outboard motor has a fuel tank mounted on the engine, it is not enough to empty the tank completely, or to fill the tank with fuel and fuel stabilizer. A half-full fuel tank is trouble. You must get the fuel out of the engine before any long-term storage. Gasoline turns to a sticky, gooey varnish in about 90 days or less. Left over the winter in an outboard motor, the gas-turned-varnish will clog the carburetor. All engines should be 'fogged' before long term storage. This procedure can be found on the fogging oil can or the engine manual. This process rids the engine of gasoline and coats interior engine surfaces with a protective oil. If you don't fog the engine, you may be in for costly repairs.

When you take an engine out of storage that has not been properly stored, even replacing old fuel with new, changing the plug(s) and spraying the carburetor with a cleaner, the varnish will cause problems. The motor may start, and it may even run at idle, but it will run poorly until an extensive cleaning job is done. If this is the case, unless you are mechanically inclined and can follow a repair manual, take the motor to a professional for the needed repair.

Assuming you did everything right when you put the engine into storage, you should still change the fuel filters. On smaller engines where the fuel tank is attached to the engine, find the filter by following the fuel line from the fuel tank to the engine block. You should encounter an in-line fuel filter which should be changed. Make sure the arrow on the filter, is pointing in the direction of the fuel flow. Use only the type filter recommended by the engine manufacturer. On larger outboards, with a separate fuel tank, follow the fuel line where it enters the engine cowling, to the block. That's where you'll usually find the filter. Check your owner's manual for directions. On inboard engines, in-line filters can also be found by following the fuel line from the fuel tank to the engine. There may be a filter where the fuel line enters the carburetor.

If you did not check the propeller shaft in the fall, do it now. Check for excessive wear on all parts, check the propeller for damage, and don't forget to look for fishing line wrapped around the shaft. Whenever working near the propeller, make sure the engine ignition switch is in the off position. On smaller engines make sure the lanyard, attached to the emergency stop switch for normal operation, is disengaged to prevent the motor from accidental starting.

While checking around the anti-cavitation plate, examine the sacrificial, zinc anodes to be sure they are at least 2/3 of their original size or replace them. Outboard engines use zinc anodes to prevent corrosion on submerged outboard motor parts. Zinc anodes are mounted to the bottom of the transom of larger boats. The corrosion process begins when two different metals are put into salt water, brackish water or polluted fresh water and electrolysis takes place. The harder steel bolts react with the softer aluminum housing or aluminum propeller, which then deteriorates. The zinc anodes will corrode in place of the parts they are protecting, thus the term, sacrificial. When in question, replace them.

Replacing oil in the lower unit of an outboard or I/O drive is easy. Use only marine oil manufactured for that purpose. Make sure the motor or the I/O lower unit, is in the running position. Place a drain pan under the lower casing. Remove the lower drain plug first, then remove the upper drain plug. Oil will then drain out of the lower hole. If water is present in the lower unit, the oil that drains out will be milky in color. If you discover water in the lower unit, you must find the problem before you operate your motor. Water in the lower unit can cause severe, costly damage.

If everything looks good and the oil is not milky, you're ready to add oil. To replace the oil in the lower unit, simply inject the specified gear oil into the lower drain plug until the oil starts to come out the upper drain hole. Insert and tighten the upper oil plug, then, quickly, remove the oil fill container from the lower drain hole, insert and tighten the plug. Even if you did change the oil in the lower unit before storage, check the level when you take it out of storage. Treat inboard engines the same as you would your automobile engine when it comes to checking and changing the motor oil. Because there is little room to drain engine oil from an inboard engine, you may want to let a qualified boat mechanic do the job. Mechanics use a suction pump that can draw engine oil out of the oil pan. If you are really into performing this function yourself, you can purchase a hand operated pump and do the same thing. Oil in some smaller inboard engines can be drained in the conventional manner by removing the oil drain plug on the bottom side of the oil pan. Use caution so oil does not spill into the bilge. Special shallow pans are made to fit under the boat motor for draining oil. Replace the oil with marine grade motor oil according to the engine manufacturers specifications.

Trailer Boats -- *Alex Zidock, Jr.*

Unless you drained all water out of your outboard motor cooling system before storage, you could experience a problem with the water pump or impeller when you put the motor back in use. Water pump impellers are made of soft, rubber material and set in the housing so several of the blades are folded over. Left this way for extended periods, the blades take a set and will not return to their original shape, loosing their ability to pump water. To overcome this during long storage periods, many owners pull the start cord a short distance periodically during storage. By moving the pistons during storage periods, the piston rings won't remain in one position for an extended time. This prevents marks on the cylinder walls. However, if you are storing your outboard where freezing temperatures occur, you may be causing a bigger problem. When you pull the start cord on the smaller outboards the impeller also moves, and the soft impeller blades will tear if ice is present in the pump. Follow the engine manufacturers recommended procedure when preparing your outboard engine for long term storage, particularly if the boat will be stored where freezing occurs.

There are two types of water cooling systems used for inboard engines. One type is much like the automobile self contained engine system. Water and coolant, circulates through the passages in the engine to keep the engine cool. You can check for the proper amount of coolant much in the same way you do when you check the automobile coolant. The other system is a raw water cooled system which uses a pump to draw raw water into the cooling jacket that cools the engine. This system continually draws in water and then dumps the heated water overboard through a fitting in the hull. Often the passageways will get blocked and will cause overheating problems. At least once a year, this type of system should be pressure flushed. Some inboards use a combination of both systems. Few if any inboard diesel engines use the raw water system.

If you start your outboard motor and notice no water is coming out of the water pilot or water discharge holes, shut the motor down as quick a possible. On some motors, it could take as little as 15 seconds to cause the engine to overheat and the pistons to seize. No flow or a weak flow is usually a good sign the water pump impeller is not working properly, or simply the pilot hole or discharge hole is plugged.

If the holes are plugged, a straight heavy paper clip or stiff wire can be used to poke the holes clear. If that doesn't solve the problem, removing the lower unit to replace the impeller is the next step. This is not a difficult task and most backyard mechanics can change an impeller.

If your motor has an electric starter you should check the gear on the starter for wear. Older motors may have starter problems, if you hear strange noises as you engage the starter to start the engine. If it's a starter problem causing the noise, the noise will disappear when the engine has started.

Battery cables should be checked, terminals cleaned and battery tie-downs securely fastened.

Every engine should have the oil and filter changed and a tune up each year, more often if it is run year-round.

Your primary checkup before you put your outboard motor into service after storage would not be complete without a general tightening of the nuts and bolts. I/O's and inboards should be gone over the same way. Caution should be taken not to over tighten bolts, as damage may occur to gaskets and seals. Bolts fastening the head to the motor should only be tightened with a torque wrench. Motors mounted permanently to the transom or a motor bracket need special attention to insure vibration has not elongated the mounting holes. Also check the nuts and bolts. Smaller, more portable motors should be mounted by hand-tightening the clamp screws, and a lock passed through the holes in the clamp handles to prevent the clamps from coming loose during operation.

The best place to start when putting an engine back in service is when you are preparing the engine for storage. What you do then will have a huge affect on how easy it will be to get your engine running again.

All the experts agree the best tool to keep your boat motor running properly is the owner's manual. By following the instructions breaking-in a new engine, winterizing and re-commissioning you can enjoy countless, trouble-free hours on the water.

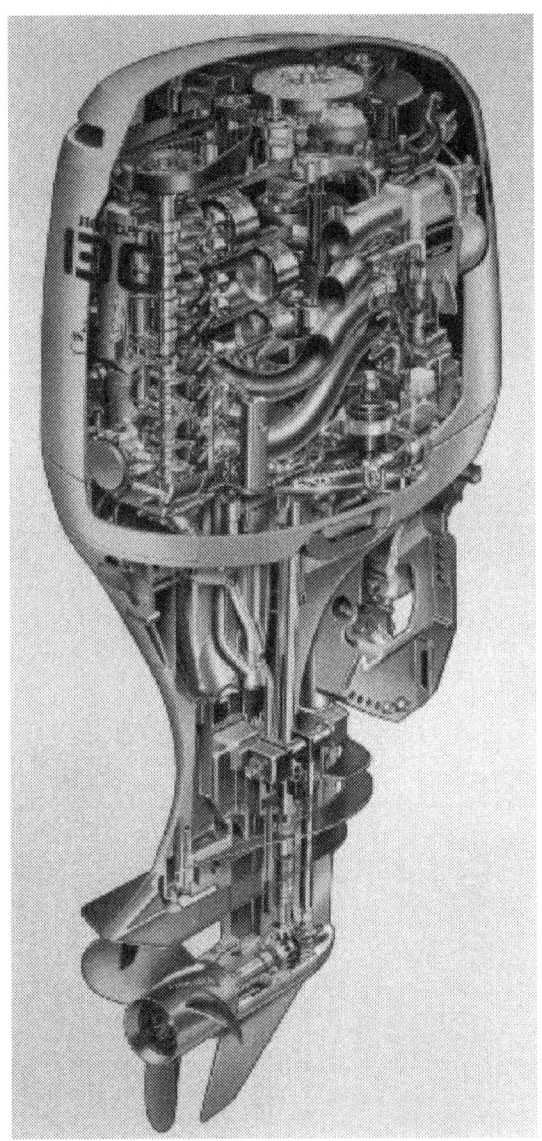

Figure 27
Courtesy of the manufacturer.

One look at the cutaway view of this engine and it becomes obvious why proper storage and care are so important to the longevity of any engine.

Trailer Boats -- Alex Zidock, Jr.

CHAPTER NINETEEN
STORAGE
SHORT & LONG TERM

A happy boater is one who has little trouble re-commissioning the boat after it has been in storage. If the boat was put away properly, putting it back into service will save time, money and frustration. It would be unusual for a trailer boater to put the boat into long-term, in water storage. Most trailer boats are stored on land, which is the best place.

It's important in any climate to take steps to store your boat and motor properly, if the boat will sit idle for more than 30 days. Refer to the chapter in this book on gasoline and it is easy to see any gasoline engine needs specific care for short or long-term storage. In most cases, the engine owner's manual will describe, step-by-step, the process to prepare the motor for storage.

The rest of the boat also needs care, to insure it will work properly when put back into service.

Boats stored in freezing climates must be prepared to deal with expansion and contraction of water trapped in the boat or motor.

When a boat is put in long-term storage, it's because is not going to be used. The ideal place to store the rig is in an out-of-the way place in the backyard, behind the garage or alongside a, seldom-used, vacation home. however, this presents an ideal setting for theft.

When you put your boat in storage, make sure you take steps to deter someone from hitching up and pulling away. Most trailer hitches have holes where locks can be installed. As an added precaution, run a chain through the holes in the wheels and around the frame of the trailer. Unless the boat is very small, it's unlikely someone will take the boat off of the trailer to haul it away. You can be sure a thief won't overlook the goodies an unsuspecting owner might leave aboard his boat. Easy to sell items like radios, televisions, GPS units and other electronic are an easy mark. Binoculars, fishing gear, ski equipment, life jackets and other odds and ends could be tempting. All should be removed.

Read your owners manual and other sections of this book on engine care and storage. Put stabilizer in the fuel, change the oil in the crankcase and lower unit and fog the engine. Replace the antifreeze in all the appropriate places, if your motor is the type with a raw water or closed water-cooling system. With the engine complete, let's move to the boat and trailer.

If your trailer is properly matched to your boat bottom, the best place to store your boat is on its trailer. There is nothing wrong with a trailer with rollers for long-term storage, but, the trailer must fit the boat properly. A boat trailer with insufficient rollers, or rollers placed in the wrong areas can cause damage to the hull. The best time to adjust this, is the last time you haul your boat out of the water before storage. The boat should be straight, with no unusual or obvious pressure points.

Bunk-type trailers support the hull over greater areas and, therefore, offer a better cradle for long term rests.

The bottom of the boat should be cleaned with a marine cleaner that will not scratch the gelcoat or the aluminum. In the north, boats are not usually put into storage until the weather gets cold. That's not the best time to apply wax. Near the end of the boating season, a month or so before storage, may be the best time to wax the boat bottom with a good, marine-grade wax.

After you find a location to store your boat, make sure the bow is pitched a little higher so water will run out of the drain hole in the transom. Trailer tires last longer when raised off the ground by supports placed under the axles and the tires covered.

While you may not have a large area to store a boat, motor and trailer indoors, it is important you take the accessories off your boat and store them inside. Electronics, as long as they are in a dry place, can be stored in an unheated garage. Things made of plastic and vinyl should be protected and may be stored in a cold area. Again, you don't want to put these things where they will mildew or get so cold they crack if bumped.

When you have all the accessories off of your boat you'll have more room to look around. Check the wiring and wire panels. Spray them with a moisture-absorbing product made specifically for the purpose. Use lubricants with Teflon to spray steering cables, throttle linkage and other moving parts that may seize when not used for a long period of time.

The winter, or any off-season, is a great time to redo the lines on your boat. If you have the time and patience, whipping lines is an interesting and rewarding pastime. They look great when you pull up to a gas dock. Lines should be taken off the boat and checked for fraying and wear, and replaced as needed.

Before you cover your boat, you should perform some preventative measures on your boat trailer before storage. Each wheel should be removed and repacked with a good, marine wheel bearing grease. Now's the best time to check the wheel bearings, brakes and general condition of the wheels. Replace the wheels and check the tires for wear.

Most trailer lights fail to work because they get corroded and lose their contact. Lenses covering lights should be removed and a small amount of grease put on the gasket. If you find the contacts corroded, use some bronze wool or fine sandpaper to clean them before you apply grease to the bulb base.

Douse the wiring harness with anti moisture spray. Use a Q-tip to clean out the sockets and then cover it with a plastic bag taped around the wires. Tape the dangling end of the harness to the trailer frame.

The hitch coupler can also be greased. Smear it inside the cap and around the ball-catch, making sure threads get covered. Check the safety chains and, if your trailer is equipped with brakes, make sure the cables work free and grease them.

A general inspection and repair of your trailer now will go a long way when you finally get to hitch it up again and head down the road.

When all the operating systems on the boat and trailer are complete, it's time to begin the cover-up process. Tilt the motor down for storage. Larger outboard engines and sterndrives require, you do this while the battery is still in the boat.

First, you want to put the regular boat cover on the boat. If the cover comes with an engine cover that's great, but if not, use a 6-foot x 6-foot plastic tarp rated for the outdoors. Use bungee cords or a short length of rope and wrap it around the engine just below the motor box. It's best to let the tarp hang so air can circulate under it to prevent moisture from building up in the engine cowling. The long parts of the tarp will protect the shaft of the engine from rain and snow. Make sure it's fastened securely, so it won't blow off.

Use a sturdy tarp and wrap the entire boat. In the north where snow and ice are a problem, a tent built over the boat will allow ice and snow to run off. Take whatever measures of protection you can to protect your investment.

The alternative to preparing your boat for long-term storage is to pay a marine dealer for the service. When you consider the cost of your investment, and the professional care it will be given, it may be the better alternative. The dealer can winterize and shrink-wrap the boat. Your only involvement is writing a check and towing it home.

Storage protection is not complete without the paper work. Many insurance policies on boats do not cover damage from ice or freezing. Check your policy for a storage rider and make sure the premium is paid in FULL.

Trailer Boats -- Alex Zidock, Jr.

CHAPTER TWENTY
A TO Z - TERMS AND TIPS

ANCHOR

There are several different types of anchors. The most popular anchor among trailer boaters is the Danforth, or fluke. This anchor does not rely on weight to be effective, instead it is constructed so the flukes dig into the bottom to hold the boat. It's important to understand why it works so you know how it works.

The anchor is attached to the boat by a line called the rode. Nylon line is the best material for an anchor rode. A six-foot piece of galvanized, vinyl coated chain should be attached between the anchor and the line rode.

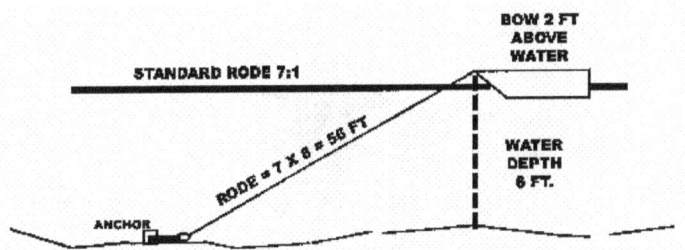

THE TOTAL LENGTH OF THE ANCHOR LINE AND THE CHAIN IS THE RODE. THE SCOPE IS THE RATIO OF THE ANCHOR RODE TO THE VERTICAL DISTANCE FROM THE BOW OF THE BOAT TO THE BOTTOM OF THE WATER.

Figure 28

The length of the rode is determined by the water depth where the boat will be anchored. In protected waters, the rode should be at least seven times the distance from the water's bottom to the deck of the boat. In rough seas, the length should be ten times the distance. In either situation, the minimum length carried should be 200-feet. This allows a 10:1 scope in 15-feet of water, with the bow 5-feet above the water.

As the fluke anchor is lowered, pressure from the rode is put on the anchor shaft, at about a 60-degree angle, which causes the pointed flukes to dig into the bottom. When the shaft of the anchor, which is where the chain is attached, is raised to about 90 degrees, the anchor flops over and is easily retrieved.

Another type of anchor is the mushroom anchor, which looks like an up-side-down mushroom. This anchor works well on small boats, in calm waters, and is preferred by owners of inflatable boats since it has no points which can damage the float tubes.

The plow anchor is bigger than the fluke, and while it is very effective, it is usually found aboard larger boats and yachts.

The yachtsman's anchor is the most familiar style. It is the heaviest for its holding power and is rarely used on any size boat today.

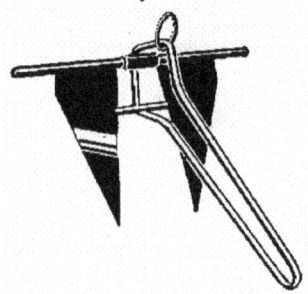

Figure 29
Open shank Danforth style anchor.

Figure 30

Plow anchor.

Figure 31`

Modified mushroom anchor.

Figure 32

Yachtsman's anchor.

BLOWER

Blowers are necessary on boats with inboard or inboard/outdrive (I/O) motors, housed in closed compartments on boats. Gas fumes are very dangerous and can collect in the bilge, or motor compartment of the boat. The blower is an exhaust fan that removes fumes from the enclosed, motor compartment.

Before starting the boat's engine, always turn on the blower for 5 minutes or more. After fueling, the blower should be run and the engine compartment and cabin areas opened to determine if there is an odor of fuel. If you smell fuel, do not start the engine until you determine where the smell is coming from. You must eliminate the problem and the odor before you attempt to start the engine or turn on any electrical switch.

COMPASS

Even if you never expect to run your boat out of sight of land, you should have a compass on your boat and know how to read it. A compass is an instrument that lets you know what direction the boat is headed. The magnet card on the face of the compass always points to magnetic north. The card is divided into 360 points, or degrees. If your compass reads 0 or 000 you are headed due (magnetic) north. If the card reads 180 degrees you're headed due south. When a heading is written, either in directions or on a chart, it is always written in three numbers.

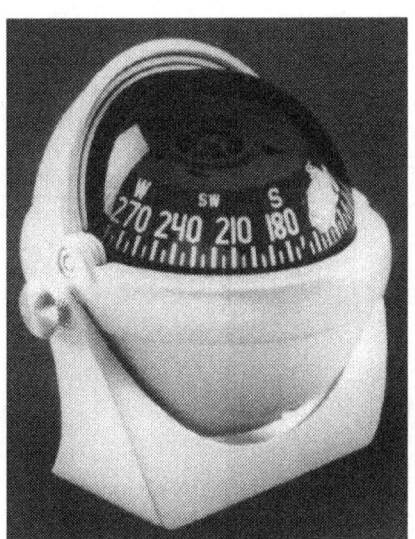

Figure 33
Courtesy of the manufacturer.

A good compass will be built well and have a sun cover.

The compass itself should be mounted so it is

directly in front of the boat operator, and in a position that makes it easy to read. A lighted compass really helps, and the bigger the compass dial, the easier it is to follow.

There is a line on the outer dome of the compass called a lubber line. If you want to head due east, you turn the boat until the lubber line is in line with the 090-degree mark on the face of dial.

You may experience deviation in your compass. Mounting your compass too near metal objects or wires can create a magnetic field and cause deviation. Never place any metal object within two-feet of the compass. A professional can adjust your compass for deviation.

If you get involved following a chart with a compass, you will soon see the compass points to magnetic north, while the chart is marked off in lines which correspond to geographic north. The difference in degrees, which could vary drastically depending on where you are, is called variation. You can determine the variation by looking at a chart. If your directions call for you to follow a true course, then it's a simple matter to add or subtract the variation from the magnetic reading.

DISTRESS

If you get into trouble with your boat, you should know how to get help. Depending on how serious the problem is, there are methods to let the Coast Guard or other boaters know you need help.

If you have a marine radio and are boating in waters patrolled by the Coast Guard, you can turn to channel 16 and call the Coast Guard direct. In an emergency where life and/or the vessel, is in immediate danger you say:

:

"MAYDAY...MAYDAY...MAYDAY"

State your boat's name, the problem and give the best location you can.

If there is immediate danger, but not life threatening, then say:
"PAHN-PAHN...PAHN-PAHN...PAHN-PAHN"

State your boat's name and the problem.
If there is a problem you want to make other boaters aware of in your immediate area, say:

"SECURITY ...SECURITY ...SECURITY"
You pronounce this word SEA-CURE-A-TAY

This would be to warn boaters of a large object floating in a channel, some other danger or an approaching weather condition.

There are also flags, flares and dye markers to use during daylight and night hours. Flying a flag upside down is another distress signal you can use if you do not have a radio or in conjunction with the radio. It's a good idea to keep all your distress materials in a waterproof container, clearly marked and easily accessible.

EDUCATION

Knowing the correct way to do nautical functions adds fun, enjoyment and safety to boating. To get a jump-start on education, the best place to turn is to the U. S. Coast Guard Auxiliary, United States Power Squadron or Red Cross classes and courses. There are even courses on the Internet. Most states have safe boating classes run by state boating divisions. You can find out how to contact these organizations through a local boat dealer, marina or the Internet.

Figure 34
Courtesy of the manufacturer.

Hand held flares must be carried on most trailer boats.

FUELING

Most trailer boaters find it more economical to top off the fuel tank in their boat on the way to the launch ramp. Usually gas prices on the water are much higher. It's a lot easier to fuel your boat on land, than on the water. However, with a few precautions, fueling on the water can be safe and easy.

After your boat is securely tied to the fuel dock, shut off the engine and ask your passengers to get off the boat. Make sure no one is smoking, and if the galley has a burner, make sure it is turned off. It's always best to handle the fueling process yourself. Every fuel dock attendant can tell you some real horror stories about people sticking the gas nozzle into air vents, fishing rod holders and fresh water fills, and pumping before they realize the mistake. Gas tank fill covers are plainly marked. You should be the only one to loosen the cap and make sure the fuel goes into the proper place.

Before you begin fueling flowing, make sure the filler nozzle is in contact with the filler outlet. This prevents the possibility of a static spark between the nozzle and the fill pipe.

The fuel tank should never be filled to the top. Filling the tank to the top can cause fuel to be spilled into the water, and there must be room for expansion.

When fueling is completed, run the blower for at least five minutes. Sniff the engine compartment, cabin area and the bilge. If you don't smell gas it's safe to start the engine.

If your boat is equipped with portable gas tanks, put the tanks on the fuel dock before filling.

Fuel spills should be cleaned up as soon as possible, making sure the paper towels or rags are disposed of properly. For large spills, don't attempt to do it yourself. Get professional help immediately. Under no circumstances, should you attempt to start the engine or turn on any switch. Do not dump bilge water mixed with gas into the water.

GROUNDING

If you use your boat, you will run aground, or hit an object in the water that may disable your boat. By using common sense and good judgment, you can prevent serious damage to your boat and your passengers. This is where a depth finder is invaluable. If you know you are heading into shallow water, you can slow down and proceed with extreme caution.

In the ocean, wood can come from almost any source, including other boats, crab pots, lobster traps, pilings, piers, logs or trees. Unfortunately water soaked wood floats just below the surface of the water and is difficult to see.

When you run aground (when, not if) or hit flotsam in the water, assess the damage as soon as possible. The damage may not be evident at first, so it's important to proceed with caution after a grounding incident or running over something. Once on the trailer, you'll be able to give the hull, lower unit (or propeller shaft) and propellers a good examination. Check for bends and nicks. If any are found, have the prop repaired or replaced before you run the boat again.

HORN

You can't use the same horn etiquette on the water you use on land. Blasting the horn three or four times in your automobile usually means you're upset at another driver or pedestrian. Blasting your horn three times on your boat means you're putting your engine in reverse. Most inland trailer boaters don't have a VHF radio on board. Captains use their horn to communicate with other boaters and to signal their intentions. Unfortunately, most operators of small boats never learn horn signals. For your own benefit and safety learn the horn signals. Here are some more common ones:

When you meet another boat head-on, you should signal your intentions. If you intend to pass in the proper way, you send one short blast, which tells the other boater you are going to turn slightly to starboard (right) and intend to pass port side to port side.

If you find it necessary to pass on your starboard side, two short blasts will alert the other captain of your intentions.

When you approach another boat from behind, and intend to overtake that boat, the signals mean the same as if you are passing bow to bow. One blast means you intend to keep starboard, overtaking on his starboard.

By marine law, you are not to proceed until the other boater responds with the same signal. This assures he understands your intentions. As I said earlier, most boaters do not know horn signals, so you may wait a long time for a horn response.

If you see danger that another boater may not, or if you want to draw attention to another boater that some danger exists, give him five short blasts on your horn.

When you approach a drawbridge, stop your boat, give one long blast and one short blast to alert the attendant to open the bridge. The bridge attendant will acknowledge with the same signal before he opens the bridge.

ICW

The Intra Coastal Waterway runs from Maine to Florida and around the Gulf of Mexico, deep into Texas. Many boaters who want to travel the East Coast without going into the ocean use this protected waterway. The ICW is well marked, the channels are maintained, there are charts available and many services are available boaters. It is advisable, the captain of a small boat be well experienced in boat handling before any extended journey.

JET DRIVES

Some outboard motors are equipped with a jet drive. The lower unit, gear case and propeller, are replaced with a unit that draws water into an impeller and forces it out a small opening, which propels the boat with a jet of water. The boat is steered by moving the nozzle from side to side. Reverse is accomplished by diverting the water in the opposite direction. The jet drive is popular in shallow water, but it has disadvantages. The jet drive requires more horsepower to reach the same speed as its prop driven counterpart.

KNOTS

Being a boater means you must learn to tie at least a few knots. You don't have to learn to tie a lot of knots, but there are some that will keep you and your expensive investment secure. One of the first knots to learn is the bowline (say bo-line). The bowline takes the place of many other knots and it is easy to tie. I learned the bowline during my first safe-boating course. It's served me well.

You can remember to tie the bowline by remembering a simple phrase. "The rabbit came out of the hole, ran around a tree and went back into the hole." You must remember the end of the line is called the bitter end. To tie the bowline make a "hole" or loop, and pass the bitter end (rabbit) through the loop and go around the line (tree) and back into the hole. A little practice and this becomes easy, quick and secure. It is a versatile knot that will do a lot for you.

Another good knot to know is the hitch. The hitch is easy and the double hitch is two hitches. Just remember hitches need constant pressure to work well.

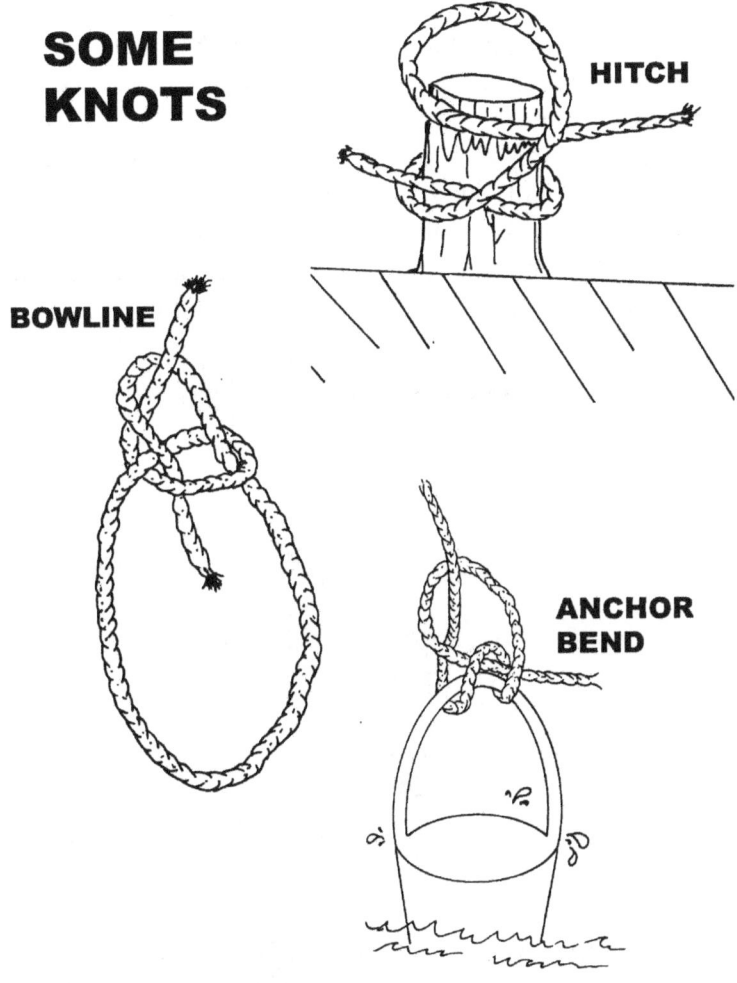

Figure 35

A few useful and easy to tie knots.

LIGHTS

Running lights are standard equipment on recreational boats. However, from time to time, boat owners must repair lenses or bulbs. The most common lights on trailerable boats (Actually, regulation on boats 39.4 feet and under) are the two sidelights at the bow of the boat which is half red and half green and the all-around, white light at the stern of the boat. As you sit in the boat facing forward, the green light will be on the right (starboard), and the red light will be on the left (port). At the stern there is one all-round white light. Lights, like horns, are a way of communicating with other boaters.

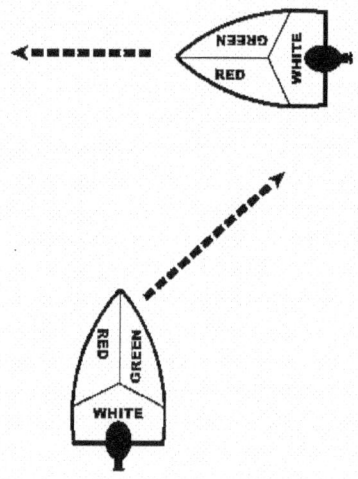

Figure 36

When boating at night, it's important to know where other boats are and in which direction they are moving. If you see a boat crossing your bow from right to left, the crossing boat (called the stand-on vessel) will show a red light. You must turn to avoid a collision.

(You are called the give-way vessel). However, if the boat is crossing your bow left to right he will show a green light. You then are the stand-on vessel and you will have the right of way. Again, always assume the other boater has not taken a boating course and does not understand the rules of the road. Avoid a collision at all costs.

MANEUVERING

Boating requires you understand how waves and water work to move your boat from one place to another. Those places include getting into or out of a docking situation. Using wind, water and lines you can put your boat in any position. Here are some situations and the proper approach if wind and tide are not factors. Drive slowly.

NAVIGATIONAL AIDS

When you are on the way to the boat ramp, the myriad of street signs and signals register in our minds as second nature. We pay attention to them without thinking, and drive accordingly. Markers are used on many of our inland waterways. You must learn what they mean and how to read them.

Maps are called nautical charts. Charts tell boaters where channels and navigational markers are located. While every attempt is made to keep markers where they belong, they do move or become damaged.

By observing the colors of the buoys, you will know which direction you are traveling. Boating courses teach they three R's — RED, RIGHT, RETURN as a method of remembering which mark should be on which side. This means if you are returning to your home port (the numbers on the marks are increasing) from the sea, the RED buoys will be on your RIGHT when you RETURN. another is: Johnny LEFT PORT with a RED nose. This saying gives you even more information. It translates when you LEAVE your home PORT, and you are proceeding seaward or down stream, the RED markers will be on the LEFT side.

Other navigational aids mark the center of the channel, speed buoys, danger buoys, mooring markers, no-wake zones and many others. The best way to learn the navigational system is by taking a safe boating course.

OUTBOARD MOTORS

An outboard motor is exactly that; the motor is outside of the boat's hull. Most trailer boats have outboard motors. The outboard hangs from the transom. Outboard motors range from 2 horsepower to more than 200 horsepower, and are built in two-stroke and four-stroke designs. Many large boats used to fish the oceans have two motors. If one engine fails the other will bring you back to port.

Twin engines burn more fuel but are easier to maneuver around docks. Boats with two motors are equipped with counter-rotating props. As viewed from the stern, one propeller rotates clockwise, while the other rotates counterclockwise.

Smaller boats used on inland waters may have two engines, but one is usually much smaller than the main engine. You can use a 90 hp as your primary motor but it's not always efficient to run that motor all day at trolling speed. Boats used primarily for fishing can add a 9.9 hp "kicker" for trolling and to provide a ride home if the main engine fails.

PERSONAL FLOTATION DEVICES
(PFD's)

Everyone on board the boat should wear PFD's. However, this is not a law. What is required is that every boat must carry one wearable life jacket (type 1, 2, 3 or 5) for every person on board and one throwable type 4.

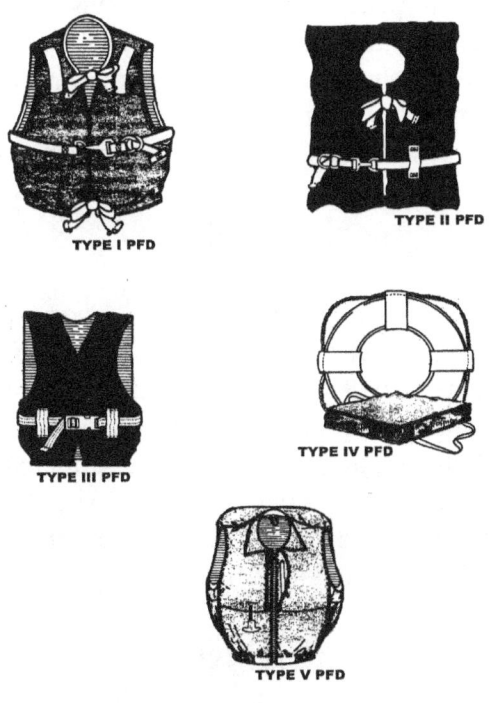

Figure 37

The five types of PFDs.

There is a difference between types of life preservers.

Type 1 is a wearable jacket that will turn an unconscious person face up in the water.

Type 2 is a vest that also will turn a person face

up. This type is used primarily in inland waters.

Type 3 is normally worn by people in active watersports like water-skiing, wakeboarding and other water toys.

Type 4 is throwable, like ring buoys and buoyant cushions, not meant to be worn.

Type 5 is heavy-duty, floatable coats, special sailboat harnesses and other hybrid vests.

Children and non-swimmers must wear PFD's when onboard, and particularly, when the boat is in motion. PFD's should be kept close at hand and easily accessible to all on board.

Always purchase Coast Guard approved PFD's.

RAFTING

Rafting is a popular practice among trailerable boats. The boats are tied, or rafted, together in protected waters where waves and wind are at a minimum. This activity, when done as a planned rendezvous, usually means all the participants know each other and enjoy each others company. There are times when dock space is at a premium and boats are rafted off the dock as a matter of accommodation, rather than a social gathering.

SKIING

Water Skiing is a popular activity among boaters. The serious water-skier may purchase a boat specifically for this sport. Water-ski boats are usually inboard boats whose hull design creates little wake. On the other hand, there are boats designed specifically for wake boarding, a very fast-growing, popular sport requiring a boat that produces a large, controlled wake.

Beginners find, after little practice, it's easy to get

up on a pair of water skis. The important thing to remember is that the skier cannot verbally communicate with the ski boat. Therefore communication is done through hand signals.

TRIM

Boats are made to operate efficiently when on plane. As a boat sits in the water motionless there is no motion effect on the hull. When the boat begins to move, water pushing against the hull, begins to affect its movement. As the boat moves at low speed, the engine causes the bow to rise and plow through the water. As speed increases, hull design and power push the bow over the bow wake, raising the hull to planing attitude. As long as speed is maintained, the boat rides on the water, with only the back half of the hull in the water.

To more effectively control the attitude of the boat, the engine -- or a hull using trim tabs -- may be angled up or down. If an engine is trimmed down too far, the force will push the bow down into the water and the boat will "plow." If the trim on the engine is too high, the force of the propeller will push the stern down and the bow up. When using the trim on the engine, make adjustments slowly, as changes in trim will definitely affect steering. Some trailerable boats are equipped with trim tabs affixed to the bottom at the transom. These tabs offer more control trimming the boat. Again, it is necessary to experiment, slowly, to determine where to set the tabs for the best, most efficient ride.

UNDERWAY

A boat is underway when it is not tied to a dock, shore, is not at anchor or hard aground. If a boat is moving forward under her own power it is said to be making headway. If the boat is going backward it is making sternway. If it is going to one side or the other, it is making leeway.

VENTILATION

If there are burning fuels the danger of Carbon Monoxide poisoning exists. If a motor is running, consider where the exhaust is going. A boat traveling 5 knots with a 10-knot tail wind will have exhaust in the cockpit.

Engines are run to keep batteries charged or to generate electricity. Some boats have electric generators driven by their own motors. Boats with enclosed areas must have ways to prevent the possibility of carbon monoxide poisoning caused by exhaust gases.

Cabins and enclosed areas should be vented and engine compartments should have power vents. Make sure all vents are open and power vents are working before each outing.

WAKE

One of the most important rules of the road is responsibility for the wake of your boat. The wake is the waves, or disturbed water your boat makes as it moves through the water. It's the turbulent, rolling water you leave behind. If your wake causes injury or property damage, **you are liable**.

XEROX

Make copies of your float plan and give it to more than one other person who is not on the trip with you. If you are late to arrive at your destination, this person knows your plans and where you might be located.

YIELD

The most important action when you are pulling a boat on a trailer. With today's smooth-riding rigs, it's easy to forget you are pulling a boat. You can't pass as closely or turn as sharply. You must yield and allow more room for the maneuver when you have a boat in tow.

ZINC

Outboard engines, as well as the hulls of larger boats, are fitted with zinc anodes. On outboards, look near the propeller and you'll see a silver colored piece of metal held onto the engine with a screw or two. On larger boats, the anodes will be placed at the stern, below the waterline, and on the running gear or outdrive. These are called sacrificial, zinc anodes. Electrolysis takes place in salt water, brackish water and some freshwater areas. In this situation the weakest metal (the zinc) is attacked first, thus protecting other submerged parts from corrosion. Never paint the zinc or paint between the zinc and its mounting surface.

Trailer Boats -- Alex Zidock, Jr.

Trailer Boats -- *Alex Zidock, Jr.*

CHAPTER TWENTY-ONE
TOOLS & EQUIPMENT

If you're not handy with tools, no matter how sophisticated your toolbox may be, the tools are useless. If you really want to be safe afloat, take a simple beginner's, mechanics course at your local community college.

Figure 38

An engine shop manual is the most important tool to have aboard.

The best tool any boater can carry is the engine owner's or an engine shop manual. I have suggested to boat owners, they invest the $25 or $35 dollars in an engine shop manual for their specific engine. Don't leave the dock unless both manuals are on board.

Unlike keeping tools in a box in the trunk of your car, every boat should have a waterproof toolbox with an assortment of the basic tools such as, locking pliers, needle-nose pliers, two sizes of crescent wrenches, a ratchet and a set of sockets in either (or both) SAE and metric sizes. Be certain it includes a spark plug socket and a good assortment of screwdrivers, both slot and phillips.

Be prepared for a quick fix, which allows a safe return to port, and the assistance of a professional. That's when supplies such as bailing wire, duct tape and electrical tape are a must. Before each season, go through the marine toolbox to add or remove items.

It's good to have extra spark plugs, belts, hoses, hose clamps and fuses on board. You must also have the proper tools and knowledge to make the repair.

This is when a good relationship with a marine dealer can pay off. Most marine dealers hire brand certified mechanics. If you buy a $12,000 outboard, the dealer will take an hour or so to do an orientation. If you buy something less expensive the dealer may not go over the product thoroughly. It is not unreasonable for the customer to pay one of the dealer's technicians for an hour to get a wealth of information about the motor. You can make a deal with the dealer that the price of the boat also includes one hour of his mechanic's time to thoroughly go over possible problems and the repair. Take notes and keep the notes with your operator's manual. If you have a failure on the water, you have some knowledge of how the engine operates and where to begin troubleshooting.

However, as motors become more sophisticated, they have the ability to warn of impending failure, allowing the boater time to head for shore. In certain cases, computers in motors can make their own internal adjustments to keep the engine running. One advantage available today is the cellular telephone, if it has the phone number of your local marine technician in its speed dial.

Being safe on the water still boils down to being prepared with spare parts, the right tools and the knowledge to use them.

Trailer Boats -- Alex Zidock, Jr.

Trailer Boats -- *Alex Zidock, Jr.*

Books Published by Bristol Fashion Publications

www.wescottcovepubishing.com

Boat Repair Made Easy — Haul Out
Written By John P. Kaufman

Boat Repair Made Easy — Finishes
Written By John P. Kaufman

Boat Repair Made Easy — Systems
Written By John P. Kaufman

Boat Repair Made Easy — Engines
Written By John P. Kaufman

Standard Ship's Log
Designed By John P. Kaufman

Large Ship's Log
Designed By John P. Kaufman

Custom Ship's Log
Designed By John P. Kaufman

Designing Power & Sail
Written By Arthur Edmunds

Fiberglass Boat Survey
Written By Arthur Edmunds

Building A Fiberglass Boat
Written By Arthur Edmunds

Trailer Boats -- *Alex Zidock, Jr.*

Buying A Great Boat
Written By Arthur Edmunds

Outfitting & Organizing Your Boat For A Day, A Week or A Lifetime
Written By Michael L. Frankel

Boater's Book of Nautical Terms
Written By David S. Yetman

Modern Boatworks
Written By David S. Yetman

Practical Seamanship
Written By David S. Yetman

Captain Jack's Basic Navigation
Written By Jack I. Davis

Captain Jack's Celestial Navigation
Written By Jack I. Davis

Captain Jack's Complete Navigation
Written By Jack I. Davis

Southwinds Gourmet
Written By Susan Garrett Mason

The Cruising Sailor
Written By Tom Dove

Daddy & I Go Boating
Written By Ken Kreisler

Trailer Boats -- *Alex Zidock, Jr.*

My Grandpa Is A Tugboat Captain
Written By Ken Kreisler

Billy The Oysterman
Written By Ken Kreisler

Creating Comfort Afloat
Written By Janet Groene

Living Aboard
Written By Janet Groene

Simple Boat Projects
Written By Donald Boone

Racing The Ice To Cape Horn
Written By Frank Guernsey & Cy Zoerner

Boater's Checklist
Written By Clay Kelley

Florida Through The Islands What Boaters Need To Know
Written By Captain Clay Kelley & Marybeth

Marine Weather Forecasting
Written By J. Frank Brumbaugh

Basic Boat Maintenance
Written By J. Frank Brumbaugh

Complete Guide To Gasoline Marine Engines
Written By John Fleming

Complete Guide To Outboard Engines
Written By John Fleming

Trailer Boats -- Alex Zidock, Jr.

Complete Guide To Diesel Marine Engines
Written By John Fleming

Trouble Shooting Gasoline Marine Engines
Written By John Fleming

Trailer Boats
Written By Alex Zidock

Skipper's Handbook
Written By Robert S. Grossman

Wake Up & Water Ski
Written By Kimberly P. Robinson

White Squall
The Last Voyage Of Albatross
Written By Richard E. Langford

Cruising South
What to Expect Along The ICW
Written By Joan Healy

Electronics Aboard
Written By Stephen Fishman

A Whale At the Port Quarter
A Treasure Chest of Sea Stories
Written By Charles Gnaegy

Five Against The Sea
A True Story of Courage & Survival
Written By Ron Arias

Trailer Boats -- Alex Zidock, Jr.

Scuttlebutt
Seafaring History & Lore
Written By Captain John Guest USCG Ret.

Cruising The South Pacific
Written By Douglas Austin

After Forty Years
How To Avoid The Pitfalls of Boating
Written By David Wheeler

Catch of The Day
How To Catch, Clean & Cook It
Written By Carla Johnson

Trailer Boats -- Alex Zidock, Jr.

Trailer Boats -- Alex Zidock, Jr.

Trailer Boats -- Alex Zidock, Jr.

About the Author

Alex Zidock, Jr., has been a freelance outdoor writer/photographer/broadcaster for nearly thirty years. Currently he is the host of "Out in the Open," a weekly television outdoor talk show that airs in Northeastern Pennsylvania. Alex is a contributing editor for Boating World magazine and a regular contributor for Pennsylvania Angler and Boater magazine. He has published articles and photographs in major boating, hunting and fishing magazines. His work has also appeared in non-outdoor publications such as Popular Mechanics. Alex has owned more than a dozen boats, most of which he towed along the East Coast. He, his wife and two children have toured most of the United States in three different motor homes. Alex fishes from Canada to the Keys.

After spending twenty-three years at a suburban Pennsylvania newspaper, Alex and his wife JoAnne launched their own advertising and public relations company in 1982. He taught photojournalism part-time at a local community college and hosted a weekly outdoors radio show for several years. He and JoAnne published Eastern Boating newspaper for five years. They ran their 30-foot boat, *Another Story*, out of Barnegat (NJ) Inlet until they closed the advertising agency and moved permanently to their vacation home on Lake Wallenpaupack in the Pennsylvania Pocono

Mountains in 1990. JoAnne sells real estate in the Poconos and helps with the television production where she appears as a frequent guest espousing the female perspective on the outdoors. They boat, fish and hunt together.

Alex is a past president of the Pennsylvania Outdoor Writers Association and a long-time member of the Outdoor Writers Association of America. He is also a past president and the former Executive Director of Boating Writers International, Inc.

www.ingramcontent.com/pod-product-compliance
Lightning Source LLC
Chambersburg PA
CBHW032254150426
43195CB00008BA/450